Time
Shadows

Like the tide, as our world turns,
visions, memories, our dreams,
things we build upon, touch our
feelings. We hear new sounds,
find new ways, they move our
lives each day. Such, goes the
glory of our world.

Charles P. Russ, Jr.

**Original Poetry of
Charles P. Russ, Jr.**

Published by:

HEADLIGHT PRESS
6500 Clito Road
Statesboro, Georgia 30461 (U.S.A.)

Cover Art Provided by *Fotolia.com*

ISBN: 1-58535-270-5

Dedication

I dedicate this book, to birth of
a moment, life's grace. New born,
our fifth generation. Lo, our great
grandson — ***Charles Joseph Russ***.

To Dorothea:

My mind rides wings of the wind.
Happy, I will never be lost in the
memory of tears. For the love we
share will stand forever and a
day.
Such, in noble song I sing. You
have made all our lives worthwhile.
In truth, you are the sunshine of
my existence.

Charles

Contents

****

Dear Reader:

I see life, as a walk through time,
space and motion. What touches
us most, the silence, the mystery.
In reflection, what moves us more
than the love feeling?
And what is more natural to a story
teller than to dream. Magic fills the
air, voices ride wings of the winds,
lo, blossom new words and purest
thoughts.
Imagination, a poet's pen, new plots
unfold, we hear new sounds, we find
new ways. A few planned lines, time,
life, nature and we, the people, walk
in a new direction.

C.P.R., Jr.
2014

PART ONE

Sonnet I—Life

Can it be, life will be what it will be.
Oh, a mystery, a wilderness we walk.
Lo, baffled, my mind speaks to me,
Our grace, we can reason as we talk.

We are not a flower, a bird or a bee.
Part of nature, creature, large, small,
Yet, we can turn rivers, sail the seas.
Oh, how we think, we talk, best of all.

We, the people, are special, you see.
Our path, our footsteps are not hollow.
We live our life free, as free can be.
Our lifelines for others there to follow.

Oh, listen, be it a city, town or a farm,
Think smart, life's truth is marching on.

Life's Connection

My eyes upon a rainbow sky, miles of
ocean wide, the breath of life touched
me. I ask, "Oh, life, who am I, why am
I here?" Of you, paths we walk, what
is my connection?"
You are so much more than a dream.
Who can I call and how can I get your
attention? My concern, so much I want
to know of time, space, motion and we,
the people.
What of togetherness? Some of us fly
the winds, some like plume-less birds.
There is laughter, tears, our loneliness.
It came out of the silence, very positive
voice.
It was not the sun, stars, of nature. Lo,
it was of life's glory lights. Sudden-like,
as if life speaks to me, I realized our
life was designed for us to understand
the sum of all things.
Oh, people, it is of the Spirit within me
that I speak. He is the One who opens
my world, shares my feelings. He is the
One, opens my heart and mind. Ah yes,
He is the One, who tells me how best
to live my life.

Of Life, I Speak

Takes trees, a brook, wild flowers, birds,
to make a forest. Takes a school, church,
a corner candy store, people, to make a
city, a town. It takes a need, a desire to
inspire a mind to think, a heart to care.
Takes emotions, our sensitivity, impact
our feelings, move our lives each new
day.
Takes the first step, walk a mile, hope,
inspiration, trust, to believe in others as
well as ourselves. Understanding of the
risks, challenges, we must confront to
live life as it should be lived. It takes a
wise man to know all of us will make
mistakes. Forgiveness is not a sin.
How sad it must be if we live with life's
unknowns. "Who are we and why are we
here? Or, by our leave, where do we go?
Unless, we have belief within ourselves;
or perhaps, a higher power."
Surely, takes everything we have to be
well, happy, enjoy life. Lo, let us be wise!
Takes a minute to realize our life is more
than an illusion, our life is real. And though
a short journey through time and space, it
is our greatest gift. Oh, people, why ours,
never to forget, upon this earth, we have
but one life to live.

Life's Magic Question

His seat, stump of an old tree by
running brook. He embarks upon
a voyage of deep thought. Ah yes,
about lessons we learn along life's
way.
How can it be, to all who knoweth
best, unknown, how we come to
earth. Now I dare not stray too far,
in thought, I mean. Yet, our lifelines
fragile, our claiming hours, empty
space. Still, only scarecrows dare
not move.
I count our many ways, romance,
love letters from the heart. Lo, old
but broad in view, mountains, the
fields, morning dew. Think! There
must be something more to this
life.
Why I must walk life's fields again,
to think, reason, how and why. Oh,
one precious thought: "Life's Magic
Question." Oh, who can tell of life,
flowers, trees, birds, the bees that
all might understand,
"Of our time, the castles, the Kings,
Why the difference in all things and
the heart and mind of man?"

Whispers From The Soul

Came from heart of the man more
than a plea. He told what promises
of life mean. "Unless we live vows
we pledge, what will breed our life
support?"
Tells, once reason calls our name,
our days and nights will smile upon
us. We learn about good seeds. Lo,
fold our arms around family and our
good friends.
Embrace them, only then, can we
build relationships, bearing walls,
the house we live. And the songs
we sing together, how we find the
harmony in life.
Such, our garden grows, so grows
beauty of the garden of life. Once
our melodies linger, we will find life's
grace. Ah yes, of such things, good
music plays.
I will never forget his words: "I am
not a judge or part of a jury. Yet, my
ardent desire, pay homage to life's
happiness. We find this, as we walk
life's roadside trails in faith, in trust
and truth." The foundation that gives
all of us comfort, lo, let us call them
"Whispers From The Soul."

Happiness

It was a day that swept my cares away,
a wise man turned my life around. He
told, we live the harmony of differences.
"How can we judge a laugh unless we
have shed a tear?"
It was afterglow of early morn, I found
the positive. Lo, happy voices, dancing
limb to limb. Like laughing boys, laughing
girls, crows in flight, their spirit touched
my soul. I remember the wise man, his
voice, one of quiet certainty. Tells, what
happiness means to you, to me.
A vital feeling we can't time or measure,
just happens. Once it runs free around
us, enters our shadow box, quiet place,
stored for all our tomorrows. And what
greater gift as we walk highs and lows
of life's roadside trails.
Once we reopen our shadow box, awake
time shadows, memories of life's fun and
games. They enter the heart of it all, life
we live, spread emotions, thrills that only
happiness can bring.
Our grace, how we dwell a happy house.
I speak of family, confluence of friends,
the joy of laughing, and what more than
the enchantment, the ecstasy of a laugh,
dare we ask of life?

About Totems

After the prayer, found he was a leader
of men. Yet, what he said, I remember
him most. Aware, my interest in Totems,
tells, as a poet turns his pen, we must
understand why the totem. It was much
more than a carving.
Story it tells, speaks from the heart. Lo,
why it must be in the heart of the man
who listens. Totems speak of all things
that matter; that give meaning to our life.
And one who listens, must be prepared
to speak for himself.
Totems are symbols, signs of the past.
Yet, help design our lives for the future.
They ignite our spirit and tell how best
to live our lives. How best we build our
relationships. Lo, we dare not bargain
with the truth.
Seems, we were made for each other.
Our life, a drama, a plot and only time
tells when we no longer stand naked
as before. Lo, we have lived. Perhaps,
on Angels wings, the way of all flesh,
we leave for an unknown land.
A time we realize we cannot hide from
ourselves. We listen to echoes, sighs,
our goodbyes. They tell us life is real.
"Why we must do something to mean
something to all who follow us."

A Special Kind Of Feeling

Walking the high road, how tall trees
hover o'er forest lawn, sun's golden
lights flashing, shadows dance upon
the hill. Lo, grows a special kind of
feeling.
As if curtains open wide, in long view
from the hill, spy gray clouds. I hear
rolling thunder. The rhythm, the pitter,
patter, beat of raindrops falling, grows
a special kind of feeling.
And the afterglow of early morn, red,
leaves, the green, the gold, lo, others
turning brown. How they cover all the
ground. I sense beauty, warmth, the
life we live. Grows a special kind of
feeling.
It was the distance, the dark clouds,
the cold, winter coming soon. Ah yes,
the coming of our day's decline. I turn,
wonder, "Who controls the life we live?
As before, unanswered. My mind spins,
my heart cries, "Oh, tell me, am I being
ignored?"
I bow upon my knee, speak in silence.
Oh, what grace, sweet Autumn morn.
I found my answer there. Yes, I found
my faith. And grows "A Special Kind
of Feeling."

Trumpet Blues

We cry harmony, yet, we live like two
sides of a hill. One all white, the snow
falls down. The other, leaves all brown,
where golden sun shines down. How
we live, we walk and we talk, has been
the magic question.
Oh, let us listen to the marching song.
One wish, we learn how to play our part.
When the band plays, all of us join the
chorus. Lo, it seemed to come from
the garden.
Was louder, louder than before, brown
eyes roll, brown fingers tap the keys.
Oh, we want to believe, all the world is
listening to the birth of, "The Trumpet
Blues."
Your call comes down, gutsy, whirling,
twirling, notes. Your cry, loud and clear,
you swing your magic horn in praise.
And it was said, one day we will find
the way to clasp hands. Oh, no more
searching.
We will all walk and talk and sing one
great song, "Togetherness." And the
golden sun will shine on both sides of
the hill. Lo, we have found our strength
through life's grace, our peace, and our
love.

Father And Son

Something about a pond, couched by
tall trees, color green. Oh, what grace,
a father, spending time with the light
of his life, his son. The fish lazy, father
shares notes he borrowed from winds
of time.
Tells, as a young man, how the song
of life came to him. "What values will
you hold?" He searched the land, sea
and the sky. One morn, met the winds
of time. How pure the sounds, music
to his ears.
Words he will never forget, words that
touched his heart. "In life, if we have
the will, we can find the way. Be wise!
The learned man knows about seeds
of life. The wise man knows how best
to plant the seed."
He told how time is measured by our
desire, promises we keep, happiness,
by our labor and our love. He turned,
asked life's magic question: "Are you
prepared to allow goodness to follow
your heart and mind?"
Tell me, are you satisfied in what you
heard? The young boy smiled, "Yes, I
am." His father sighed, "Ah yes, today,
a young boy became a man."

Lights From The Soul

He called it morning mischief.
Once awake, two voices speak to
him. Happens when the shadows
of doubt enter his life, walk upon
paths he walks.
They play twist, turn, parry with
choices he is called upon to make.
Lo, they affect the paths he walks.
His concern, how his mind greets
the terms life offers. How his heart,
always plays a part.
Where does he place his trust?
How beautiful, the sounds of life.
How the mind reasons, questions
the risk. How his heart measures
the values, lends reason to the
will of moderation.
In reflection, the power of choice
given to man. Oh, like the mighty
tree, we can adapt to all seasons.
Our grace, he calls them, "Lights
From The Soul."
A mind that can think, reason, how
and why. A heart that can moderate
the choices, we are called upon to
make.

Song Of Friendship

I speak, merging of paths, how it binds
two hearts, How once we crown our path,
the hand of a friend, it molds character
of our soul. And once they clasp hands,
positive steps bring us together. Lo, all
things seem positive!
Sudden-like we realize, mere words not
strong enough to define a friend. Think!
Who else will hold a hand, add to growth
of time? Lo, if ill winds blow and builds a
need, a friend will stand like mighty tree,
never bending.
Though he may speak softly, his strong
sense of longing. He will find a way to
reconcile the pain. When hill snow defines
our path. We stand, two leaves hugging in
the thaw. A friend will stand by, despite
inclement weather.
Whatever may unfold, the hills to climb,
the rivers to cross, all things belong to
the "Song of Friendship." A friend will
find the way, navigate rivers and climb
mountains of our tomorrows.
Listen, listen, what more breeds peace
and more content than faith in a friend?
I speak of one great truth: Lo, one will
never have the need to walk life's path
alone.

On Wings Of The Wind

"Our world turns, we learn something new each day." Speaks to me, how we sense so much in life. Yet, how we still stand in silence, from whom and from where we came. Lo, and why we make the tour.

As time turns, we, the people, seem to live in a house of glass. Less and less seems to matter. One by one, many of our memories shatter. Lo, we seem to ignore how far we have come in this world of ours.

One thing certain, we need each other. And what is more beautiful than to find our life is like poetry in motion. Ah yes, we learn where the heart is. Such was the day, bursts forth wise words upon the running winds.

How passion can fool us, our heart and mind in freedom roam. How we all learn mere words are not enough. There is a companion to their time, the deeds that follow. Oh, dear friends, let us think and think again.

Lest we invoke caring through both our words and deeds. Words will silently fly away like the Mocking bird in flight. Oh, none but whispers, "On Wings of the Wind."

Fences

Oh, what serenades life more than
the gift of fellowship, family and our
friends. How when happiness calls
or clouds collapse around us, cries
sadness, feelings rise, move our
lives new found ways. I remember
how it happened to me.
Their place, large brick house, long
driveway roundabout, a fence along
the way. It seemed foreboding, yet,
something about a fence. Not too
high, not too low, a dividing line or
a place for a friendly chat, pass the
time of day.
Now good chats will develop good
neighbors, and good neighbors soon
become good friends. And let us pay
attention to the swinging gate: open,
time for a friendly chat, if closed, time
for the dinner bell.
One day, good friends may come to
say goodbye. How fortunate, when we
build good fences. A place stories are
told, retold, and friendly chats will soon
become memories we will never forget.
In truth, they will become treasures of
our time.

Ode To A Teacher

A morn, rich and rare, when green
grass gave life's meaning to me. Ask,
"What influences our life more than a
teacher?" It was beauty of her words,
how unique our world, many cultures,
how we come from everywhere. And
about birds, white snow, forest green,
we, the people, fences and little white
houses. Oh, so much more!
Memories my thrill, I can still see the
little white schoolhouse upon the hill.
How she tolls the bell, lo, warning call,
to every little Jack and Jill: "Oh, please
do not be late, come to the little white
schoolhouse upon the hill."
Her high top shoes, a long white gown,
summer's breeze. Soon autumn leaves
will come falling down. One becomes
so aware how many winds have blown
down. Ah yes, how many masks of time
have passed this little town;
Yet, the bells still toll; lo, grass still green
all around. My eyes still see her in a long
white gown, still trim and fair, her legacy,
found everywhere. "Come one, come all,
together we will inherit the earth, sky and
the sea. Oh, my Dear Children, my mind,
my heart, will always be open to thee."

The Night Owl Cried

Walking backyard country, drifting
winds, horns, bells, people sounds,
noises of the day. Where they may
roam, cannot always tell. It was the
deep throat howl of the train, found
his message.
We are but passengers on streets
of time. "Why are we asked to face
the many challenges life offers? And
what of life's contradictions? How we
are born? Why do we die?"
Forever a dreamer, notes how time's
rhythms never seem to change. And
he wonders if time renews itself. Ah
yes, is forever. Asks, can it be, once
we reach end of our cable tow, we
too, renew ourselves?"
A moment, the night owl cried, turns,
he asks, "Lo, is this the dream I have
been waiting for? One day, we leave
this place for the hidden village, the
center of all things?"
Where time and space lingers, we all
meet again. Why, "The Night Owl Cried?"
A warning sign, a loving sign, how life
is so fragile. "We are so soon here, so
soon gone, somewhere along the way."

The Family Tree

We were so young, youth on the run.
I remember the sound of Chapel Bells,
how we all gathered round a Holy man;
silent man, a stern man, story he told.
How from nature, a mighty tree grows.
Nurtured by sun, misty rain, grows as
if lifelines in flight, limbs spread far and
wide.
Such grows the style of man; one day
severed from the vine, born, little child,
member of the family. Once nurtured
well, like a little bird, spreads his wings,
searches new paths to travel. Some
of us search our roots, others search
far beyond. One day enlightened, find
our place on streets of time.
Lo, solemn our need, never forget our
roots, "The Family Tree." Indeed, a call,
a visit, send a letter. Oh, people, above
all, keep in touch. I will never forget the
Holy man, wisdom of his words, and the
question he asked of me:
"Are your knuckles bare from helping all
those who have climbed the tree? Or,
perhaps, those who may be sliding down?"
Oh, a day I learned, "Life is about others,
not all about me."

Faith Revived

His path long, walks the dawn, aches
and pains. Aware his path a downward
course, tells how once born a Prince.
One day, we stand like an old tree, the
winter, snowbound.
Aware he had reached the better part
of knowing time, asked, "From where,
from whom, do we find the strength to
labor and to love?" Unanswered, path
of leaves his pillow, he stakes his claim
upon a little boy's smile.
Out of the silence of forest morn, from
a distance, sound the mellow tones of
his Grandson: "Grandpa, where are you?
You are my friend." He turns, he listens.
The tempest that shakes an old man's
mind disappears.
Like a rising tide, his life stands before
him. Grace grows memories of family
sounds, grasps his part of time, "He is
the wheat, I am the chaff." Oh, as if
lightning strikes, light of the full moon,
his eyes no longer dim.
Oh, something real happened to him
that day. He found life's one great truth,
cried, "Oh, people, 'My Faith Revived,'
my Grandson. I will walk the rest of my
life through him."

Roaming Field

Awake, I greet the shadow lights of
dawn. Enters my mind how we rise
upon the sun, spread forth upon the
land. People in the roaming field, life
of which we swiftly glide.
Our first steps, walk our path, search
promises to keep. Lo, without thought
who made them, chop trees, build our
house, snip flowers, grace our table.
We seldom ask where else they play
a part.
I see birds, creatures large and small,
how close we are. Yet, how we stand
unknown. How in silence we speak.
I wonder, can it be we live in a fool's
paradise? Sudden shock! The voice
I heard.
"Listen, from whom, from where the
call, man is above all? Can you see,
one day, he too, hangs ice needles
upon forest trees, Oh, what else but
a journey ending?"
My surprise, the wonder of it all. I turn,
on bended knee, call upon one I hold
most dear, "Oh, Great Mystery Power,
can you tell why life's secrets elude us?
And can you tell why you play tricks in
the "Roaming Field?"

Silence, Be Thy Word

They were two fine men, yet, their
voices loud. Neither one in doubt,
how we should think or move within
our world about. It seemed absurd,
two men of great renown; morals,
ethics, the proper way to treat our
fellow man.
Oh, who can tell, can anyone be so
absolutely sure? Oh, I find it difficult
to know! In the garden of religion,
they teach noble ways, while there
are noble ways, indeed. Diverse as
we may be, all of us don't care for
garden plants; others, allow birds to
eat the seed.
Why, I ask of you, What's in a name?
Else, path we travel by. And when we
speak, like a lion's roar, the strength
of every bridge we cross, surely, key
to open many doors. Oh, people, listen,
hear me now:
My way has been, do not preach to
others, nor tell them what beliefs are
so, but to establish guidelines, within
myself to know. Lo, let silence be my
word! And if by my actions, my deeds,
I succeed, surely then, my voice it will
be heard.

When In Silence We Speak

Edge of dawn, his place high upon the
hill. One by one, lights go on, he spies
shadows moving, the multitude, people
far below. Silence, all around him, lo, the
mystery of our world about touched him.
Cries, "What or who moves our world
each new day?"
As if by instinct, bows his head, bends a
knee, speaks in silence. Oh, a quiet time
when our heart and mind come together,
share their feelings. Precious moments,
when we can see life in more than one
dimension.
Light, darkness, our seasons, how we
laugh, we tear, love, we hate. Oh, hard
to believe, across the hill, lonely sound,
the tower bells. Softly, softly, drifting the
winds, voices in song. It was the melody
and how it lingered, he speaks.
How centuries we have questioned the
end of time. How we cry for help, follows
the doubt, the sadness, lo, the unknown.
Yet, who knows but for life's grace what
grief has passed us by. Or, how many of
us no longer lost but have been saved,
"When In Silence We Speak."

Feelings

Toll of old clock upon the wall, talks
to me, how time walks in silence; lo,
each second a shadow, each minute
a memory. One precious moment, I
mix memory with desire. I see life in
all its splendor.
I remember, it was a Father and son;
a real life situation. "Father, are you
much too bold? How you wear your
feelings on your sleeve?" Lo, softly,
softly, his Father answered:
"My son, think about life and how best
we measure happiness; the thrills we
find along life's way. And tell me what
you think moves our lives each new
day. Our eyes that see, ears that hear,
or lips that speak.
"Oh, how do you know me?
"Else awake each morn, the wind, the
rain, the sun, my color burning bright.
"Lo, a song in my heart! Listen, listen,
hear my call."
I speak of relationships, one to the
other, love, romance, lo, all things. I
ask you now and then again. "What
is more noble than to pay homage
to what moves our lives each new
day, our "Feelings."

One Precious Wish

It came upon wings of a dream,
quiet voice: "What is a good life?"
In spirit of it all, answered, "Once
you walk in the right direction, lo,
love, the foundation, as is giving,
caring, sharing."
How will you find the good life,
once you live your life with what
you have been given? It will find
you. How do I begin my quest?
Think!
No matter how little life may offer,
we must do something important
with our lives. Speaks to me, how
firm the knots we tie. Oh, there is
our pride, our house, family, our
family of friends.
When life is no longer a balloon
on a string. Love, our life is our
everything. And from what I see,
one precious day, time will call
my name,
Like an old tree, my body stoops
in sigh. Oh, "One Precious Wish."
I look back and cry, "Lo, to all you
people in my life, how fortunate
can I be, the life I lived, belonged
to me."

A Call To Arms

How golden lights break gray dawn
through windows of the trees. I wonder
of their dwelling place. Perhaps, there
is another world? Oh, to understand life
and how to measure time?
Touches me, words of a Holy man, how
our day begins once the shadow lights
of dawn call our names. How we open
windows of our world. Lo, through our
feelings, happiness or tears.
A day, I let my thoughts run free about
we, the people, some rooted and some
restless. How to each other we must
be prepared to give and share. Oh, let
us understand life and time.
How each one of us reach the better
part of knowing time; leave this place.
Why? Unknown! Yet, about the quick
and the dead, the silence? Thereto,
their lives had meaning.
Why we must never give up the doing,
the thinking about our life. Such, shines
the golden sun, the good times. Or we
sail the gray sea, the bad times. Let us
think joy, speak joy and happiness, will
give life meaning. Ah yes, will follow us
all the days of our lives.

The Story Teller

He tells of a beautiful garden in the
center, placed the presence of man.
His gift, a world that offers a path of
new discoveries. Lessons we learn
along the way, harness your dreams,
follow the winds, study the curtains
of time.
Tells, life like two sides of a hill, one
loud, clear; the other, of boundless
silence. About we, the people? The
wonder of it all. How we live, we walk,
we talk, we play together, we learn
how to live together.
Moments, the story teller, stood quiet
and still. As if a ghost came down, lo,
soft voice, thought he heard before.
"Be wise, beware shadows of dawn.
Reconcile, learn to live, with what life
has given to you."
It was said, the old man, the listener,
turned, speaks, "Lo, perhaps, one
day, veil of silence will be lifted. We
find we are more than wayfarers on
streets of time. Given reason to think,
the how and why. Lo, reason tells me,
surely there must be something more;
else, why were we born?"

PART TWO

Sonnet II

Love Is

A broad brim, a flower or two,
Damsels strutting in the park.
Chic little hat, with veil of blue,
Coming soon, song of the lark.

Happily, a time of windy days,
Flocks, pretty birds flying above.
Maidens skirts blow tricky ways,
Young man's fancy turns to love.

Like two birds, the same feather.
Two happy hearts clasp hands;
And they agree to walk together,
Till called upon to leave this land.

Lo, pretty girls, birds on the wing.
Portend, our love is our everything.

One Magic Moment

Alone, with his thoughts, as if life's
music plays. Old time tunes spin his
mind. Remembers how two hearts
meet, they share golden hands of
friendship.
Life turning, turning, suddenly, life's
fancies rise, flame their souls. They
saddle wings of a dream, lo, passion
plays a part. Cry intimate thoughts, a
maiden's voice.
Oh, something new, she stands alone
there for him. Something divine, how a
thousand horses cannot separate two
happy hearts. Swift as an arrow strikes,
born, truth in love.
Enters their brave new world, welcome
fire; vows they take and promises they
make. I speak of life's truth; a little bit of
Heaven called their names. They agree
to walk the same direction.
Oh, one solitary life, one love; love bold,
love kind, love dear. Oh, people, tell me,
what greater gift, "One Magic Moment,"
two happy hearts, agree, time to share
a crown. Their love, faith, trust, forever
and a day.

Love Has An Affair With Life

How do we know love? What is more
thrilling than a pretty girl's smile, the
promise of a kiss? Lo, once two hearts
meet, agree to walk together, the rest
of their lives.
Love is a sweetheart, kind words of a
friend. If sadness walks our path, it's
found in each beat of an aching heart.
Lo, life's most precious moments, our
love is of truth and it becomes our life
support.
Once we cross the bridge of time, we
lend reason to passion. We understand
happiness is not having everything but
loving everything we have. Oh, through
love, we find the bearing wall of every
house we live.
Our grace, we walk the calming hours
of each new morn. Two hearts dancing,
singing old time tunes. A love still true,
untarnished, has become the sunshine
of our existence.
Oh, how do we know love?
When love is the first, the last, we found
happiness, we found peace. We will not
fear the last shadows of time, but we will
give our thanks, our praise: "Love Has
An Affair With Life."

When Love Is True

One often wonders of passion's call,
how subtle it falls upon the eyes of
youth. Stirs the embers of our heart;
sounds of life begin. And though our
feelings rise, sadly, often time's pale
lights speak: "She is not the one for
me." Yet, how beautiful when love is
true.
I remember, how a gift of idle hours,
flamed my heart. She wore green and
white, excitement in a tailored suit. Lo,
like a young bird, cast my eyes upon
my cat. He bends an ear, as if to say,
"Poor fool, you have failed to see the
breath of spring passing by."
Oh, from cloud to cloud, I dance with
the wind. Her golden hair, her clothes,
her style, her smile, touched my heart.
In truth, the speed of light, my eyes
followed the path she walked. Lo, one
precious moment, day Heaven called
my name.
So much more than a bird of passage,
how soon true love cried out to me. Oh,
like a little bird in song, the break of day.
I called her name, rang the marriage bell.
I dared not let her fly away.

Little Girl On A Swing

Softly breathes days of spring, turns
new greening of the wood. Unveiled,
beauty of a rainbow sky smiles upon
a little girl on a swing. Oh, what more
can breathe life's rhythm than feelings
of the heart.
Awake, Heaven's Watchful Eye, the
sun shines upon the crown she wears,
sweet face, chaste and fair. Lo, a morn
life's mystery plays a part. Out of life's
silence, the players of the pipes, wind's
sweet songs fill the air.
Dressed beyond what we mortals wear,
steps delicate, as if upon wings he flies;
garden path, to the swing. He whispers,
of what only words of love can tell. Like
nothing else, feelings rise, passions flow.
They reach life's perfect rhythm.
How sweet the afterglow, the birth of a
moment. Oh, louder than before, winds
sweet sounds fill the air. And she smiles,
she sighs, "Oh, please, come swing with
me, my sweet butterfly."

Beyond The Dream

It was the morning after our first night.
The silence, smile upon our face, two
hearts were in tune. The open window,
blue sky, meadows wide, we take heed
the order of things. Yes, our lives were
in change.
Natural, we turn to our promises made,
how we plan to dance in perfect rhythm
of our time. What is clear but unspoken,
trust and truth will be our guide. Lo, one
wish, one love, one life, never surrender,
vows we have taken.
I retreat to a mind that plays a part.
My dear, grows in my mind like blossoms
on a vine, thousand blended notes. How
we captured love's delights, sweet words:
"I—love—you." What will follow, our love
will grow and grow.
And what will touch me every day of our
lives, a light that will guide me, your pretty
face. Yet, like all things in life, silence will
call; one of us will leave, beyond time and
place. Oh, one precious wish, we will not
weep.
For our life, time honored, the sowing and
the mowing, the harvest; our happiness.
Lo, we will have been measured by time's
long frame! Our path, the one best traveled.

A Letter Home

My dear, the guns are silent now, the
dark of night, the stars, the moon, the
distance, I think of you. Lo, we are so
far apart. I ask, "What is a heart without
a friend?"
We were so young, yet, fond memories
walk shadows of my mind. I remember
how you laughed with me, cried with me,
sighed with me. Why the muffled sounds,
the guns, the silence between, speaks to
me.
Sadness all around me, loneliness, my sin.
Why I reach out to you, recall your sweet
words, "I—love—you. Here, death stings the
night. Why I long our house, the barn, silo
on the side. And the bench we share, the
path along the way."
Most of all, our secret place and what
might have been. I turn to the thousand
souls around me, they too, were young in
heart. Trees, now all bare, land all barren,
the silence, cause my heart to cry loud
and clear.
Oh, let the wishing well draw water, so
anxious am I to return. I miss you so. I
seal this letter with a kiss and honorable
words of a soldier. "My dear, I love you.
I love you."

One Joyous Morn

Softly, softly, blow summer breeze,
when wild flowers dance the wood.
I remember their jolly hearts, pretty
damsels in the park. How on windy
days, young men smile, their pretty
colors, as maiden's skirts, blow in
tricky ways.
I remember a large feather, a veil
of blue, chic little hat, perhaps a
flower or two. As two hearts meet,
as if heaven calls their name, clasp
hands. Swiftly, swiftly, we found love
has its own way of speaking.
Time turns, we reached better part of
knowing time. Like a house, old stone
wall, seldom in need of repair, grows.
Togetherness. Like little birds in song,
we sing, "Oh, happiness, how sweet
you are!"
I speak of my partner, my friend, my
love. How we celebrate the elegance
of that "One Joyous Morn." The Chapel
bells ring, we sing love's sweet song.
"My dear, I do, I do. I will come to live
in a house with you."

Flower Garden

How can it happen? Place music plays,
drinks served, we come clean shaven,
dressed for the party. We swagger, all
gather corner of the room. Our watchful
waiting. One by one, swing, their sway,
they enter, wild flowers come to the
dance.
I waste no time, seek night's challenge,
two happy hearts dancing in the "Flower
Garden." A night, fate became my friend.
Tresses gold, a body smooth, two happy
hearts dancing. Music soft and low, we
dance the whole night through.
My grace, the long walk home, our two
hearts linger. Lo, getting to know each
other, she accepts a longing heart. My
shock, her solemn cry, "Innocent." Our
new day dawning. I cry.
My dear, before you grieve, will not be
the four winds that blow. It will be only
my loving arms around thee. Lo, before
your sadness, organ's soft chords will
bleed. Our two hearts will clasp hands,
and sing one song.
"Of all the flowers in life's garden, our
marriage the effect. Oh, from now and
our forever, I will only dance with you."

About Love And Truth

He lived in a quiet house, his desires,
seldom partner to expectations, were
courting lonely sounds. As if the winds
blow, gates of happiness open. Enters,
his life, a violet, pure as a single star in
the sky.
Like rhythm of the rain, his heart beat
louder than before. Her steps soft, her
eyes bright, her look, "Come walk with
me." As if lights turned on, they saddle
wings of a dream. Out of the night, life's
music plays.
They laugh, sing, dance, how soon, find
their private garden. Life turning, aware
one day soon, not too far away, their lives
will change. He cries loud and clear, "Oh,
can you see, what our love has done for
me?"
The soft purr of her voice, she tells how
beautiful, when love lingers alive, "Can it
be like a painting, an idle ship, on ocean
wide? Can it be forever?" Softly, whispers
his reply.
"How many times can I thank you? Will
they ever be exhausted? I think not, my
storeroom, just for you. Such, each new
day, our dreams reborn. I sense truth, I
speak truth, the way you taught me. Oh,
how I thank you, and I love you for it."

Shopping For Clothes

I remember the moment, sun's ribbons
of light shine upon her picture. Speaks
to me of something I will never forget—
the shadow of her smile. A model in her
time, top of her head, the tip of her toes,
one wish, "Shopping For Clothes."
It was the train, her seat by the window,
showers of beauty, vary the beats of my
heart. Her scarf, her shoes, purse she
carried, how she ignored my stare. Yet,
her side-long glance, I knew, there was
something else there.
Momentum of the train, slower, I notice
she hesitates. I pick up the pace, smile.
It was the touch of her hand, my heart
sings. Leaves have fallen now, many a
season has passed us by. Yet, path we
walk, still upward bound, our love bold,
still have, we still hold.
In quiet of the calm, I often wonder the
splendor of our way. Hats, shoes that
she wears, our life, our time, the order
of the day, how time shadows will call
our name. Oh, tell me, what memories
will stand when the heart goes silent?
Lo, listen, listen, her picture standing
on the dresser, "Shopping For Clothes."

Love's Sweet Song

Lakeside, breathes my mind how
the wind tickles the trees. Heaven's
mist rising o'er lake water blue. Lo,
your Father's house, path you walk,
how we met. How soon life's fancies
mix love with desire.
I remember our secret place where
fragrance of pine needles touched
me. Each new day the same. I was
there, you were next to me. Slowly,
silently, our patterns of life change.
We found love.
I remember sweet call of the dove,
my cry in return, "I will forever walk
the forest path with you." Oh, how
subtle, we crossed the bridge, played
host to life's most precious words—
"I—love—you."
Of our life, we agree, we will sleep
the brave, our dream never ending.
Lo, so few angry words, our passion
filled, not one minute, one hour, our
love false.
I remember the church upon the hill,
how the tower bells rang; how our two
hearts are still in tune. Oh, listen, hear
me now, "We still sing 'Love's Sweet
Song.'"

Mother's Love

Eyes fixed upon family pictures on
the wall. Look out the window where
the past years are. Her smile, how
she planned her life for us, love my
memory.
As if Heaven smiled upon her, how
her words and deeds embraced all
our doubts and fears. House dress,
an evening gown, finds her comfort
every place she walks. Like ocean
waves shift the sand, she was our
driving force.
Dwells her heart. Love so endowed
to enrich our lives, lo, so dedicated,
only God dares command a space
between us. Blythe spirit, knuckles
bare, gloves to soothe hands rough;
finds her place in our garden.
Such was the first to welcome our
little ones; lo, first to place them
first in line. How beautiful to watch
her smile, her care, new blossoms
on the vine. And how they loved her
for it.
Oh, so bound to the place she loves.
And so aware, one day time will call,
Mother will leave this place. Forever
will live in our hearts, "Mother's Love."

Beauty, Love And Innocence

Happened, the Sabbath morn.
It was Grandpa, whispered his ear.
How in a beautiful garden, in heart
of it all, where love was born, God
made man. He also created a path
angels walk.
Of cherubic face, of twinkling eyes,
wings of softness and surprise. In
spirit of desire, they plant seeds
on paths they walk. Nurture them
with all the joys and pleasures He
approves.
Once dewdrops fall, grow flowers,
grass, trees. Invite all Mothers and
Dads, walk the paths angels walk.
How soon, life's music plays. Once
passion calls, like birds, bees, they
dance to life's music.
How soon, they find truth in love.
Lo, a poet leans upon a child's eye
view. So this story told how angels
come from God's house where all
things are beautiful.
Lo, little children come from paths
angels walk. Such, new life, all little
children are born of "Beauty, Love
And Innocence."

Our Son, Our Son

Her steps soft, her motions delicate,
first moment she called my name. I
believe words of the Psalmist, "With
Him, all things are possible." Across
the years, walks the night, my claim
to fame, like a candle burning bright,
a wife, a Mother.
Life turning, turning, came to pass,
life's music played, born of beauty,
love and innocence, a little child. Lo,
walks life's circle of light, a boy's will.
All the little things little boys say and
do. Older now, acts like a man, does
manly things.
Though we cannot judge a man's spirit
to give, to care, to share. He walks with
us, he talks with us on his own. Our life,
our time, in all things; lo, "Our Son, Our
Son." Oh, listen, listen, in him, our love,
our pride.
In the crucible of time, I have traveled
decades, decades and more, and have
heard the voices of great men. "Beyond
our needs, what is life's greatest gift?"
Oh, people, please hear my call. "Amen,
so be it, what else but through the grace
of God, born, a Son."

Joy, Peace, Love

We gather round the family room to
pay tribute to the Holy Tree. Lo, we
laugh, we sing, yet, never forget the
reverence. I will never know a more
perfect story.
Three Wise Men, their search, the
splendor, mystery, truth behind the
brightest star in the sky. Oh, my star
bright, story of one solitary life. How
it was in the beginning, interim, the
afterglow. How we pay tribute to His
love.
We place a wreath upon the door,
a candle in the window, sing of the
gift of life. And life's grace, family,
friends, the love we all share. Lo,
wisdom of his words, "Joy, Peace,
Love." How we find our happiness,
our pleasures.
Oh, something I was taught, I am
prone to believe the awe of His
presence; how we bask in peace,
not by pots of gold or garments we
wear, but style of man. Lo, positive
steps, be true to ourselves and to
others, giving, caring. What makes
all of our life worthwhile.

In Reflection

First, pitter-patter, music of the rain
happened as if the rainbow sighed,
pretty colors dance time shadows of
my mind. She was honey blonde, so
young. Lo, my anxious heart, courted
rainbow's glory, her pretty colors,
her accents pure. Flows beauty of a
virgin stream. Splendor of her swing,
her sway, as if paradise touched my
longing heart. A merchant of love, lo,
look to her pretty colors to change,
make my heart sing.
Surprise how she danced; yet, she
refused to play games young men
play. Her smile, to let me know she
cared. Her sigh, "Yes, I will walk with
you once the games you play are
now and forever."
I often wondered, perhaps a silent
hand touched me. Chapel bells, the
Deacon's words change the games
we play. Oh, listen, listen, how loud
my heart sings!
Tonight we walk city streets, towns,
country places. Our two happy hearts,
all in tune, dancing, time shadows of
our mind.

Along Old Logging Road

It was a lonely flower upon the hill,
stirs whisper of time's recall. Country
boy, a country girl and how we played
together, found pleasures that never
leave us.
How we frolic the hay loft, give life to
a very important day. Our desires, our
blushing, our life would just never be
the same. How soon, everyday, two of
us here in the gray dawn, old logging
road.
It was ours alone, our secret, the birth
of loving hearts. Oh, perhaps, our gait
too fast. Like the flower to the bee, the
pouring rain, one washed away. Ah yes,
we were too young to cry.
Older now, I stand in the garden of hope.
I want to recapture what was building
inside us. Why I fear not, I care not, I
cry out, "Where are you? Please call
my name. I miss you, can you see?
Forgiveness is not a sin."
I want to harness the thrill, the spirit
that united our two hearts. How you
held my hand, whispered sweet words,
how we embraced, ran wild together,
the gray dawn, "Along Old Logging
Road."

Tribute To Love

Our bay window, the pretty colors,
flowers, soft winds blow and how
they dance. I can feel the motion of
our time, a thousand blended notes.
Oh, it's so hard to believe we have
lived beyond the gold.
I remember the day we met as if a
flower touched my heart; the beauty
of a kiss. Oh, so much more than a
dream, grace notes, opened gates
of happiness. How soon we realize
we cannot be absent one from the
other.
We clasp hands, greet life's most
perfect day, Deacon's words, when
two become one. Build our house
with stones of care, grow a family,
milestones. As time turns, present
and past meet, continue to drink
from a cup of love.
In truth, our cup runneth over, why
I call time. We continue to capture
life's precious moments, celebrate
that one precious day our soul will
not deny. Oh, how many cries, how
many sighs, how many times can
I thank you, our "Tribute To Love,"
Our Anniversary!

Love Letters

He walks like an old man walks,
tuned to life's empty corridors;
loneliness, the guest within his
heart, clouds his mind. Why he
calls time: "Oh, time, my steps
slow, slower, where do you lead
me?"
Hard to believe light beams hang
shadows upon the wall. Shapes
and forms touch his inner thoughts.
He remembers an open fire when
two hearts agreed to walk together,
fill life's empty footsteps.
In his solitude, thinking life through,
realized, "Life is not all about time.
Life is about people, how they walk
through time." Looking back, how
best they played their part, it was
not the charm nor how they speak
to each other. It was of truth, how
they lived promises made.
He turned and closed the dresser
drawer. Awake, she called his name,
wondered why he was chuckling. He
smiled his reply, "My dear, our grace,
memory shadows, love letters from
the start. Oh, how they still thrill my
tired old heart."

Lifelines And The Love Feeling

How soft, stillness of the morn. Sun
shines, little birds sing. A morn, life's
pretty colors speak to me of time and
how love can become a never ending
thing.
Swiftly, swiftly, as if on wings of the
wind, voices fill the air, solemn words.
Tell like sailing ships, love rides highs
and lows the tides of life. Two happy
hearts clasp hands, slowly, silently we
build a sanctuary.
What greater gift, we find the love of
our life. Shout, "Why fear dark of night?
I have found a star to guide us by." Lo,
we sing, we dance, share what all the
world should know. Ah yes, we found
truth in love.
In recall, I remember, like an idle ship,
an idle ocean, love sailed with us. Ah
yes, became a never ending thing. Oh,
what moved our world? We found new
ways to harvest beauty.
Lo, we take the time to enjoy time.
We found a devotion that grows and
grows time shadows. Tell me, what is
more beautiful than fond memories?
Those we can build upon, in support
of the lifelines of our time.

I Call Your Name

Happened, a quiet morn, lonely morn,
all was calm, all was still. Head bowed,
stands by her mourning stone, speaks.
My dear, I miss you, by your leave, my
life, hauntingly still. It's time's distance
that bars our way, and why I call your
name.
I recall your sweet words in our last
goodbye, "My dear, live, enjoy the fruit
of life. I know, you will never slight my
name." He turned, cried out, "My dear,
please listen."
It was the church fair, she walks like
you, talks like you. Oh, how my world
came alive again. She smiled at me,
I smiled at her, the music played and
our steps quickened. Shock! How she
danced like you.
Why I must confess my guilt. I held
her hand. Her face, so much more
than a face in the crowd. My heart
beats louder than before. Lo, listen,
hear me now!
She touches me, places that make
me think of you. Lo, when we dance
our two hearts all in tune. Why I pray,
once Chapel bells ring again, you will
understand why, "I Call Your Name."

I Will Never Forget

The path was long. I was weary, I find
a place with a view, as if pages from a
book, memory shadows, spin my mind.
Natural to a child of winter, my dreams
speak to me, tell where all of my riches
are.
How despite our humble beginning, we
are still in love. I speak of summer winds,
two of us, one step above poverty lines.
Yet, found the way to walk a happiness
trail. Soon, not too long, found the way
to build a Kingdom bold.
Two hearts in tune, we labor, we love,
live life in all its splendor. Our vantage
point, the high road, trust and truth. Lo,
born, life's greatest gift, happiness! In
recall, one might ask, "Please, tell, how
it happened."
We were true to friends, life we lived, and
true to ourselves. We nurtured life well,
giving, caring. Of such, ever to be aware,
one must never walk alone. The way life
intended it to be.
Aware one day, I will lose all that I hold
dear. Love, of which, means all the world
to me. I will cry, "Fetch me a path of truth,
of no regret. Oh, for what I have lost, our
love, our life, I will never forget; will never
forget."

Fly The North Wind

Apprehension, how she seemed to
be resisting change, I cry out to her.
My dear, we have lived our life as if
no hill was too steep to climb. We have
never feared loss of passion's thrill,
the touch of time. Listen to a happy
heart.
I am aware time is a silent thing. We
stand in life's magic circle, icons of
old age. Yet, what fills my heart with
joy, how we still sing, dance our life
through. Our happiness, all because
we realize little things count, matter,
and they give life meaning.
Why I ask of you, "When one of us
is called upon, leave this place, lo,
why dare shed tears? Why not look
back, remember spring when love
was true and filled the air."
Call it a fantasy, call it a dream how
sweet memories, how we stood like
mighty rocks against ocean waves.
How we still stand together, enjoying
the elegance of time. Comes the call,
"Fly The North Wind," lo, I will shout
to all the world, "Oh, what else but our
love, need fly with me!"

Plea To The Flutter Bee

Decades, decades, in this old house,
memories mark the corridors we dwell.
Our eyes in long view from the hill, we
still enjoy autumn leaves that crest the
hill, winter white, the summer winds. If
one cared to ask, we still have a love
affair with life.

Why we cry, "Oh, death, we see you as
a flutter bee, wonder when we will feel
your sting. We watch your passion feed
flowers, suckle morning dew. We stand
in wonder, once the moon hangs low.
If you call, will you tell who will be the
first to know?"

Oh, we do not court you, each sting of
your touch, like a bird of wounded wing,
fly away, fly away. Silence, never to be
heard again. Why the call of your name,
our feelings rise. Our fear, loss of life's
greatest gift—Love. Think! Love is what
we live for. Love is life. In truth, it is our
life-support.

Our one wish, when you call, we leave
for a hidden village. A very quiet place,
the other side of things. A place where
we will meet again. And our two hearts
walk hand in hand, along life's endless
path.

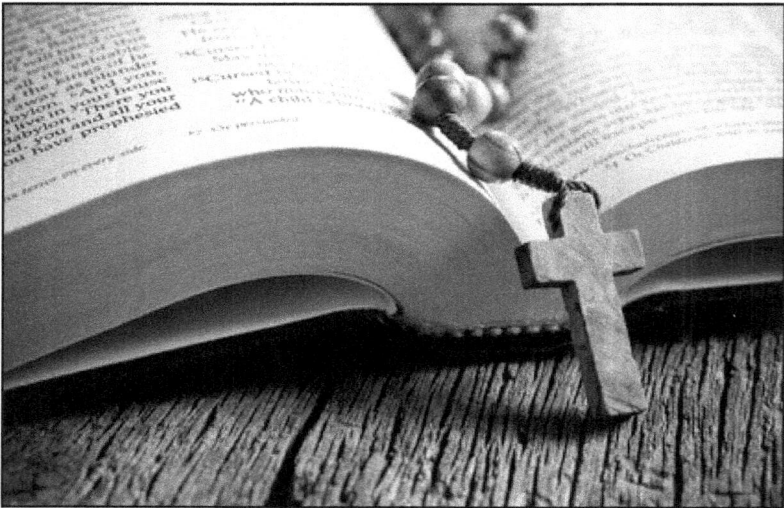

PART THREE

Sonnet III

Prayer

Awake, morning all quiet and still.
Softly, organ's soft chords bleed.
Toll the Chapel bells, across the hill,
My mind turns, new thoughts breed.

Moments, I yield to the poetry of life.
Little child born, who controls his time?
Will it be happiness, sadness or strife?
Can it be his life planned line by line?

Shock! Lone shadow marked the trees.
I turn, my sense, someone else is there.
Lo, bow my head, bend upon my knees.
My search, answers, I speak in prayer.

Oh, I call upon Him in his Holy Lands.
Pray, my soul with God, will join hands.

Life Is A Mystery

A few moments before sleep, suddenly
a star racing across the sky spins my
mind, phantoms of delight, dreams; lo,
my surprise, they share my journey, my
sense, a mystery.
How our future is bathed in silence and
life's secrets elude us. How like a master
puzzle, people some of the pieces. Who
are we? Why are we here? And birds, the
bees, flowers, nature in all its glory. Oh,
can it be that we are part of nature too?
A mystery?
Let my words be understood, no twists,
no turns their meaning. "Unlike people,
who walk, talk, reason how and why, all
things in life stand in silence. One often
wonders, the powers we received. Who
can tell, are they unique to man?" Ah yes,
a mystery!
Yet, can we too, be ones deceived? How
we might think night as a quiet time. Yet,
fashioned in night's world of silence, our
dreams. The story they tell of where we
go, when we leave this place. Lo, I must
confess—a mystery.
Softly, softly, they came drifting across the
green to my ears, loud and clear, sounds
of music. Oh, people, songs I believe that
I have heard before.

You are so much more than a laugh,
a tear, figment of one's imagination.
You were born to live. Lo, turn thee
then, let not life's silence, pomp, its
vain or useless talk, stain or mock
you.
We have been told, place your faith
along side your fears. Ah yes, there
is another side of things. A place of
boundless silence, we meet familiar
faces, sing old time tunes. Perhaps,
we are back home again, lo, where
truth stands in all its glory.
I remember thinking, if one cared to
listen to my tale, would hear my sigh:
"Ah Yes, our 'Life Is A Mystery.'"

The River Swift

My eyes in long view from the hill, gray
clouds. Suddenly, as if sound of drums,
thunder roars and sky blue's sleeves of
light, lost to reaper night. A mind in tune,
enters a melancholy strain and I wonder
about life, all things.
My search to understand, heard a voice
from deep within. Tells how our life, like
a river swift, has its highs and lows. Oh,
when new plots unfold! We hear new
sounds, we find new ways.
Often, as if driftwood, they impede our
journey, alter our course. As rivers flow,
we reach a place, the water begins to
fall; flows a weary stream. We cry out in
the night, all is still. Where it will all end,
none can tell.
Came out of the silence, this story told.
Lo, I wonder, can it be that one precious
moment, like merging of two great rivers?
A new course, no change in pace, in time
or motion?
Oh, can you see, I speak of the birth of a
moment. Like birds in song, break of day,
something new, something real going on.
How rain falls, then sun smiles, and our life
turns. Oh, within my heart, I have a new
song to sing, a new path to travel.

Oh, people, I speak from the heart.
Once we have lived, we find we were
strong enough to withstand tempest's
roar. Why not like birds, bees, flowers
and the trees, breathe easy; live, live.
Oh, once the call comes down, have
faith. Lo, be strong enough to accept
the change in the style and life of man.

Silhouettes On The Lake

Quiet of early morn, he was barely awake,
the lake, green trees, house on the other
side. Till soft winds blow, their silhouettes
on lake water ride. Oh, how he loved this
time; time to reflect.
As one by one, dew drops touch his face,
he asks, "Are they beads of happiness or
tears?" He turns, remembers a boy in his
teens. His anxious thought, knows by his
tomorrow, he will have lost his today. And
what comes with him, none but memories
of living his life his way.
He cries, "Do I see life as it really is?
In the test of time, are we not born with only
what will be yours, what will be mine?"
Oh, hear my call, Oh prideful one. You who
cry, look only to me. My mind so keen and
bright, body erect and tall. My face, charm
that will appeal to all.
You who live your life in vainglorious way,
You who are blessed, be not the peacock
in the barnyard loop. I ask you to think. Lo,
while we can hear the cock crow, he only
crows the early morn. What you seem to
espouse, cannot survive the test of time.
For we come into this life only "With what
will be yours, what will be mine."

Oh, be wise, be not like my barnyard
friend who strides in boastful delight.
For in his pride, he can see none but
himself in his own light. Fails to see
the farmer; his turn, the knife.
The sun was shining, the air was pure.
Softly, softly, as lake water rides, now
wide awake. How clear his mind, how
clear he could see the "Silhouettes
On The Lake."

Life Notes

Coming home across meadows wide,
tired, rest upon a fence along the way.
A dog barks, a night owl swoops down,
little creatures scamper the tall grass.
Touched me, man's place in the breath
of life.
How only man can speak, reason how
and why. And though we cry out, "Who
are we?" Unanswered! I have spoken
to great men, holy men, all who have
earned our respect. I have not found
the answer.
What renders pain, talk of a Deity, a
reverence; something we cannot see,
we cannot touch. The lack of evidence,
why great men cry. Yet, of such, many
of us continue to pray. Oh, so anxious
to find the answer.
Oh, to think, again to think.
Unless, through unequivocal, absolute
evidence, we cannot prove something
is or something isn't. Lo, seems a man
is a fool in his heart if he accepts what
he cannot prove what is or isn't.
It happened upon the calming hours of
the morn. One by one, counting golden
rays of the sun, suddenly realize I am
not defenseless.

I ask, "Is not a belief something else?"
And surely, we have the given right to
embrace life's most valuable gift— "To
think, to reason, to believe."
Can you see, life was not designed
for silence. In point, perhaps, in time,
one day, a miracle. We find all things
are possible. Ah yes, such goes the
glory of our world.

My Country, My Country

It is through the feelings of my heart
I speak. The place of the Blue, the
Gray. A very special land and a very
special kind of people.
A place, forever sun, land of cotton,
where a man will fight for a woman's
virtue. He stands proud, eyes upon
his plantation; his way of life. Surely,
gifts of God. Yet, there was a group
of people, hang joyless eyes, absent
their hearts, things thrilling. Why they
cried, "Freedom!"
Blow, blow the winds, freedom calls!
Blue coats come riding, tempest roars.
Blue, the Gray, brother against brother.
One day, Gray coats tattered a land
all quiet and still. My country, the pity
of it all, sadness, remorse, tears; our
land wasted.
Lo, the cries of today, what disturbs
me! Change in life, anger, remorse,
how attitudes of hate, turn our mind.
Have we forgotten His words, "Let us
love others, as we want to be loved."?
Are we blindly ignoring trust and truth?
Oh, let us not forget the Blue and the
Gray, how we all came together, and
a great nation was reborn.

What have we learned?
One thing certain, we are special
kind of people living in a special
kind of land. We are family, we are
freedom to all people who dare cry
freedom.
What does this story tell?
Never again dare we blindly ignore
trust and truth. Lo, let us forever cry,
"Freedom!" Oh, hear me now: As I
listen to the winds, if we ever forget,
it can happen again!

As A Sparrow Flies

Alone in the woods, my forest chair,
blanket of leaves. Drifting the winds
across forest green, chapel bells. Lo,
touched me, spins my mind, Deacon's
words: "In life, often little things count,
give life meaning."
I realize, my contentment comes from
earthly things. Yet, I will not turn from
life's mysteries, happenings from afar.
Hard to believe, came upon that very
moment. I spy a wildcat, profound her
paws upon a little sparrow.
Suddenly, feelings of sadness engulf
my soul. Each new flutter, sparrow's
wings, cat's hungry look, her longing
eyes, gives herself away. Moments,
out of the silence, call of a hound. Lo,
cat's ears rise!
It was her twitching nose, how her tail
curls, spells her fear. Shifts the winds,
resounding crash, a blown down tree,
breaks morning silence. Of spirit wise,
light of foot, cat leaps aside. Lo, swift
as an arrow, sparrow flies, fly away, fly
away tree top high. Oh, rendered deep
within my heart, the happenings; all the
little things that count.

How clear the air, the sound of
bells, call of the hound, the fall
of a mighty tree. My eyes upon
the sparrow, of all the tell-tale
signs. What else but let a mind
run free.
It was my vision rewards, my day.
From what I have learned, from
what I see, Of this life, all things.
I think, I think again. Surely, there
must be so much more going on.

Family Tie

The story begins beautiful and fair,
splendor of a man, a woman. Once
life's rhythms flow, two hearts all in
tune, echoes follow. Speak words,
of what only words of truth in love
can tell.
Once faith and trust rewards their
dream, grows and grows a family,
a circle of love. Time turns, life's
music plays, how soon time has
ways of speaking. One day, lost,
a member of the cast.
Often, the link that ties the family,
one to the other, a time one asks,
"Who can I call? Oh, where do we
go from here?" Moments our mind,
like an empty shell, lo, confused,
cries, "Help!"
Of questions asked, silence walks
like the night. Unanswered! Alone,
quiet light break of day, one finds
life is more than a dream. Our life
is true.
I speak of what means all the world
to one in waiting, almost lost. One
wish, we can recapture the ties that
bind. Listen, hear how it happened
to me.

I spoke to mirror on the wall, he
did not answer me. Suddenly, a
knock upon the door. I look upon
the mirror on the wall. Lo, he was
smiling at me.

I open the door, the smiles, hugs,
kisses, the sounds of life speak to
me. Lo, I cry no more! I found the
very best of me. Oh, the bond of
which I speak— "Family Tie."

Do We Stand Alone?

On the terrace, 'neath the early moon,
streaks gray and white, night shadows
stalk the evening sky. Oh, life, I stand
upon your crest, as if a tidal wave, one
day, will come crashing down. Why of
life, I speak, the flower, a tree and we,
the people.
Center of my apple field, stands mighty
tree. Old in years, still bears fruit, often
wonder why. And there, in barren unkept
garden near, a friend still stands. Once
graceful rose. These two friends cause
me to smile. For my foot on garden rail,
nooks and crannies, my terrace too, is
not in modern style.
Mighty tree, once graceful rose, I can
feel your strength in time. Where else
do you play a part? I think, I reason, no
answer can I find. Lo, I wonder here in
deep repose, of we, the tree, the once
graceful rose.
Do we have special attributes? And are
they unique to humankind? Of such, can
only we perceive the powers we receive?
Or, like minds gone on before, are we too,
ones deceived? Hard to believe, moments
sound the bells, softly, softly, organ's soft
chords weep in sigh.

I turn, upon one bended knee,
speak in silence, as free as free
can be. Lo, I praise the time we
call divine.
For I have been told in time, in
His gentle way, we will know. If
only me or we three are whole.
The time, we are called upon,
to understand the meaning of
our soul.

Lunch Money

A busy place, morning, noon, night
time too. Horns, bells, people sounds,
noises of the day. And where are all
the flowers and the trees? None but
yards and yards of cement, we call
them city streets!
Place a young boy, wears high top
shoes, V-neck sweater, color, basic
blue. To some, he walks outside the
order of the day. In truth, he walks
inside, as fire burns; has the will to
find the way.
He plays the many games city boys
play, box ball, stick ball, Johnny on
the pony. Sadly, like the gray dawn,
resembles the sadness, searches
cellars, call them basements today.
Find bottles, any old book or any
old toy.
After school, he collects old papers,
cardboard boxes, or any little thing
that has value. Sells them to the
junkyard man. Lo, it comes upon
Saturday morn, many young boys
cry, "Let's all go down to Charlie's
block. We can play carnival games.
We might win a Mutt and Jeff book."

Today, his children ask, "What in the
world were you doing?" In truth, hard
to explain, even by a young boy who
had his very own latch key. Ah yes,
in reflection, he had learned how to
live.

The carnival, all gather round, was
a penny a toss. Throw a hoop and
loop a peg. Oh, how they laughed
and laughed.

Charlie laughed too. Yet, only Charlie
knew, how important the pennies. His
"Lunch Money."

The Light In Darkness

I remember standing there, old red
barn, silo on the side, the fence in
need of repair. How it separates the
green, follows dusty lane. I can still
hear rhythm of the rumble, the deep
throat howl of the train.
I remember steel gray look, winter's
eye, yellows, reds, the orange leaves,
how they cradle the trees 'neath the
summer sky. It was there in the glory
light, came the shaker of the day. My
invitation, be different, the path I walk
along life's way.
Thus, to think, to think, ever onward
I must think. My challenge, time and
place, the reason, how and why. For
if within my heart, none but an empty
song, how will I know to whom the
place where I belong?
It was there in the shadow upon the
hill a voice within me cried, "What is
thy choice?" Oh, never let it be said,
I did not care for thee. The question I
asked of me, "What will be told if you
fail to let your spirit take hold?" Came
across the hill understanding, "Life is
a journey, one walk, a very short time."

And success and happiness is not
sameness to all. Yet, choice must
have its way. Thus, to think, again
to think.
Is it not true to respect each state
of mind, the choice of one or all? Is
the essence of nobility, like the light
that strikes darkness, the end of the
hall?

Life's Music Plays

Awake, patiently waiting for our day
to begin, singing brook, the rhythm
of the rain, sound of drums. Thunder
roars. My heart skips a beat, in one
precious moment, life's music plays.
I see life in all its glory, the land, sea,
the sky.
Our place, as if part of the audience,
in life's theater on the round where
waves make music on the sand. Lo,
mellow tones, tide's rise and fall. The
forest green, flow the sweet breaths
of spring; little birds in song.
In blink of an eye, wind blows down,
its voice sings, the highs and lows of
life. Time leaves dance, suddenly the
basso tones, winter calls and autumn
leaves begin to fall.
When we, the people, show concern.
We may hang like ice needles upon
forest trees, all quiet and still. While
we do not panic, we wonder, do we
stand in the assembly of something
we cannot touch and we cannot see?
Perhaps, a singing voice.
It was how smooth the mallards glide,
lake water rides, their little ones close
behind. I found the power of the calm.

My life came back to me, our
days, nights, our seasons, how
we live, nature, creatures large
and small; birds, the bees, all
things.
How time rotates, renews itself,
and how our hearts and minds
in freedom roam. Ah yes, how
life's music plays. Oh, why not
believe, there must be a leader
of the band.

The High Road

Making his way across the sand, cool,
biting, fragrance of sea water fills the
air. Sun shining, it was sudden-like,
as if a doorway opens in the sky, dark
clouds come down, casting shadows
upon the shore.
The surprise, sudden change, natural
to ask of life's meaning, "Will it rain?"
Lo, curious, spins his mind; how silent
life is about our future. Hard to believe,
loud and clear, tower bells ring, songs
of life come to him.
Once born, we walk as far as we can
go. No angry words or ills bar our way.
We seek new and bold adventures.
Like birds fly, we fly our time through,
Yet, our concern, we fear our destiny.
Why color our mind blue? Lo, without
choice, why not a dream?
Beyond the shadows, midnight hours
do not stand still. We greet a new kind
of time. We spread our wings, reach
out, walk "The High Road." Eyes to
see, ears to hear, voice to speak, we
clasp hands with the crowd.
Oh, how all will amaze, the whistles,
the bells, the horns, on our new path.
And the willingness, how they share
their trust, their labor and their love.

Happened, his dreams awake.
Seemed from afar, a quiet voice,
"Oh, be not a fool. How fierce the
morn, we realize how little we all
know about life.
Listen, listen, fear not the night
wind's call. Upon your leave, your
path, "The High Road." Ah yes,
you are coming back home again!

My Soldier Boy

I often wonder what provoked him to
talk. He told of a far off place, little town,
far from the place he called home. Path
he walked, a soldier's sadness, heads
low, tired, weary; like wolves on prowl,
return to their lair. From a distance, as
if thunder roars, the battle was muffled;
a soldier's snore.
They were boys, now called men, ever
aware, they were answer, a loved one's
prayer. And beyond the fear, they could
sense unholy feelings filled the air. Lo, if
one cared to listen, could hear soldier's
sigh.
"Lord, you who have done so much good
in the past, please don't fail us in the last."
He knew, as so many others had before
him, the battle was o'er. Oh, how can
we all believe such goes the glory of the
world. Do you remember when?
The sun was shining, crowds of people,
how all the banners unfurled, the important
ones do the speaking; often pompous air.
The bands play. They march to tunes we
all heard before. Some laugh, some cheer,
some tear. Yet, all feel the excitement, the
thrill. Shout, their cries of joy, "My Soldier
Boy, My Soldier Boy."

And then we cry.
How like little lambs they follow
a shepherd. Oh, look, look, see
their parched and wrinkled lips.
And then we sigh.
Why do we continue to indulge
fate? Why do we all forget the
inevitable sadness? Comes the
sounds of silence, thunder no
longer roars.
Some of us will continue to sleep,
and some of us continue to weep.
Oh, not joy, sadness, "My Soldier
Boy, My Soldier Boy."

A Walk In The West

Perched an old tree trunk, my forest
chair, how sweet the sound; hum of
the rapids, dancing brook's way. My
view, mountain green, I hail coyote's
lonely wail along mountain trails. Lo,
peace is by my side!
Dream far beyond; sagebrush green,
land of red rock hues, black canyons
too. Where burst forth, sun's flames
upon a fabled land of Anasazi, Hopi,
Navajo. If we care to listen, can still
hear their cry, "Oh, Mother Earth, of
something old, something new, this
is your land, our land too for all of
us belong to you."
I turn, the mountains, lakes, forest
green, how wind blows down, wisps
of snow, mark the land, change the
forest scene. Cause my shout, "Oh,
there must be a silent hand."
Why I kneel upon my bended knee,
give thanks, we are free as free can
be. Looking back upon this fabled
land, the human beings of the plains,
let us all hail memories, how they
paint their faces, how they ride. And
our good fortune, how peace, is still
by our side.

In recall, the lakes, feeding streams,
the desert, where the sun seems to
shine forever. Oh, let us spell life's
truth.

"Oh, Mother Earth, this land is yours,
this land is my land too; not brother
against brother, but together, like two
birds of the same feather."

Moments, a lone shadow moved on
the hill, a mighty elk stands tall, his
nose pointed toward the sky. Lo, he
sounds his mighty bugle call.

As if Heaven was in my grasp, I lift
up my head in pride, shout, "Lo, the
west, where peace is by my side!"

Honor Thyself

He was so much more than a face
in the crowd. His steadfast, steel
blue eyes, how he came forth and
answered the young man, almost
spiritual-like. He tells how our life
is real but a short journey.
How often those anxious to speak
have little to say. An ordinary man,
who was he to speak? Yet, of this
life, there are so many cares of the
day. Why we must all come to know
the talents of our time.
Think! If the peak of time we fail to
take our stand, speak truth, are we
not useless souls? Truth is golden;
the key that open doorways to the
heart. Oh, what of the man, knows
where good fortunes lead, yet, he
remains silent? Oh, tell me, should
he not be impaled on the liar's
fence?
And he who spreads scorn behind
the door in taunt of one or all, is he
not but a lackey bent on privilege?
Listen, listen, "What violence done,
once we fail the truth?" We forever
walk, crooked lips, on crooked legs;
Lo, faith's open door will be forever
closed to thee.

I speak not of confessions of the soul.
In all humility, I speak truth. Why I ask
all you people in my life, "Speak loud,
speak clear." Let us all walk a straight
path, guarded by the high walls of truth.
Lo, "Honor Thyself!" How all will know
thee, how all will call thy name.

The Picture, My Father And Me

It was hush of early morn, lonely cry
of the loon, imprints of my youth, mark
the garden of my time. Lo, wholesome
hours, hours of sweet content, grown
out of love. Lo, of memories, of which
I will never forget.
He was handsome, tall, lean, it was
time had the way, changing the scene.
Silver white on top, sits a comfort chair,
'neath tall trees. Until old man winter
calls, then chills the day and swallows
the leaves.
As I gaze out the window, whisper the
winds, each sway of a tall tree, rise the
picture, my Father and me. Games we
play, the laughs, tears, oh, not victory
or defeat. We sign our name, how best
we play the game.
Mistakes that were made, scares in the
night. Oh, no fear, my heart in his hand,
the love of this man. Lo, I remember the
pounding, the sweat on the ground. Yet,
life's grace, the elegance I found.
And now, as I look out the window, what
do I see? Oh, none but long lines in the
sky. Our sweet memories, our happiness,
our love, mountaintop high.

Now life has way of measuring our
mind. Something I learned from
sharing his time. Why I count each
new day for time has a way, slowly,
slowly, fading away.
And I laugh like a clown, how we
spelled love. Oh, what more can be
found? Now each morn I rise, I find
his chair out of sight. I look out the
window, tall pines on the right. Lo,
whisper the winds, each sway of a
tall tree, rise love, our happiness,
"The Picture Of My Father And Me."

The Price Too High

Life is a mystery, time a silent thing.
Perhaps, why we were given reason
to think, how and why. Time is real,
made for living. Oh, why do so many
of us forget?
How beautiful, how pure, born a little
child. One day, grows as a little child
should. Somewhere along life's path,
finds a place in the center of things;
perhaps a candy store.
Someone always there to sell what
hangs low behind the counter; call it
sweet stuff. He most enjoys the high
time in the garden. Lo, a mind hangs
on a cloud, he hears voices that don't
belong to him.
Once laid down, twists and turns, a
body hangs limp, motionless and still.
Awake, skin tight, none but memories
of a long story. So intense, the need,
almost lost; wonders about his friends.
How do they know him?
Once he inhales the sweet stuff, walks
like a balloon on a string. Oh, some of
them laugh, some cry. And despite it all,
the price keeps rising, like he does. Oh,
what fools we are. We know better. Yet,
we allow our heart and mind to run free.

One often wonders, when will it all
end? Perhaps, one night he stands
alone, helpless. His desire to speak,
finds he is hooked, his voice choked
still.
Oh, people, who can tell the reason
why? Indeed, all of us have been told,
drugs, "The Price Too High."

Along Brook's Way

How subtle, our spirit calls our name.
It was 'neath the hunter's moon, the
cold subdued, tree crotch matched my
hide. As I softly kiss the night goodbye,
brook's echoing waters tell, all is calm
along brook's way.
Happened, afterglow of early morn, lazy
winds come down, change the mood of
forest green. My heart beats as in song
and a new time zone in my life was born.
I become more aware of happenings, lo,
more aware of what they mean. I reclaim
memories of life, our times, places and
things.
The rivers we cross, the hills we climb,
my feelings rise, they become personal,
more emotional. How once we reach the
top we see all things through feelings of
our mind. How we connect to the loss of
a friend, a little child's cry, the plight of a
blind boy.
Perhaps, the silence, nature of the day,
I realize what marks our happiness. We
dare not forget to share a place passion
feeds, for once sorrow calls our name,
as if the quick coming of night, how swift
our mind in tune. We see all things in life,
through feelings of our heart.

Oh, something I will never forget,
how the winds came down loud
and clear, murmurs from running
brook. Tells, in all things in our life,
we must speak through feelings,
of both our heart and mind.
Oh, my enchanted forest, you who
share splendor of winter white and
summer green. While with you, the
feelings of my heart and mind came
alive today. Here, in your calm, your
beauty, "Along Brook's Way."

Merrily, Merrily Running Free

Hard to believe how little things spring
forth, become part of life's prevailing beat.
I remember Mother's hand, ocean waves
rolling upon the sand. Close by, locked in
sandy pools, tiny minnows anxious to be
free.
I let go Mother's hand, trench I dig, pool
to rolling sea. Swiftly, swiftly, water flows,
tiny minnows swim side by side, anxious
to swim the ocean wide. I groan, as surly
waves try to stem their urge, to catch the
running tide.
Sudden-like, as if touched by an unseen
hand, my feelings high. As tiny minnows
wiggle, wiggle, free at last, they swim the
ocean wide. My long view across the sea,
I turn, I realize how soon grown up, I too
will swim the running tide.
Spins my mind, the silence, I remember
my Mother's words; words I understand.
"My son, one day, you too, will be grown
up, free of a Mother's hand. Lo, laughing,
singing, dancing, like the ocean waves
upon the sand."
Perhaps, my fear of life's unknowns, my
leave, merrily running free. Something I
will never forget: how she turned, how
she smiled at me.

Ah yes, softly, softly, calmed my day.
"My son, there is a spirit in our life, we
cannot touch, we cannot see. Oh, fear
not the unknown. Like the Captain of
a ship, you will never sail alone. He will
guide you as you sail life's rolling sea,"
"Merrily, Merrily Running Free."

The Rock At Godfrey Pond

How beautiful, little child, blonde, blonde
hair, how he runs free. A Grandfather's
smile, his Grandson, polite and trim. Lo,
he knows, he will have his way with him.
Their first steps, laughing as they cross
meadows wide.
Lunch box, cookies, apples for two, then
off through the woods where the old red
house stood. Crouch low, 'neath limbs of
blown-down trees. Laugh, two of them,
walking upon their knees.
Spy remnants, the old grist mill, marks
the path, turn left, top of the hill. Opens
wide, the lake beyond, stands alone the
mountain of stone. Precious moments
when the winds blow down and life sheds
its feelings.
Little birds sing, leaves rustle in glee, the
creaking of tall trees. Surely, a little bit of
Heaven, the forest scene, the lake, the
feeding streams. Lo, stirs a Grandfather's
mind, one wish, two of us, no fears, none
but happiness, no tears.
How best to remember the years? A little
child's glory, "Oh, Grandpa, please tell me
a story." Little bit of grace, the rock, where
little elves and fairies dance the wood. Lo,
the witches fly, their brooms in the sky.

I will never forget his inquiring look.
"Grandpa, how can it be? Are you fooling
me?" Oh, bright as bright, as a Grandson
can be. Of such, goes the glory of our
world.
How soon winter comes upon us, cries
Autumn goodbye. Now all grown up, my
wish in sigh, I dare not forget the soul of
my mind. In truth, life's sweet memories,
the treasures of our time.
Stories told, his twinkling eyes, blonde,
blonde hair. Lo, my Grandson, of whom
I am so fond. Our sweet times together,
"The Rock At Godfrey Pond."

The Magic Of It All

Walking backyard country, my seat
the crotch of an old tree, memories
cloud my mind; a mind plays tricks.
I remember the old red barn, silo on
the side. Across the green, the lake,
where fish abound.
A young boy, a fishing rod beneath
green trees. Surrounds him, birds in
song, little forest creatures, romance;
squirrels dancing, the brown leaves
falling. The air, the silence, this was
his world.
His future unknown, yet, he smiles
within himself. Lo, like a little bird
prepares to leave the nest, he has
learned to be on his own. Oh, much
more than a farm boy. Life he feels,
so much more than an illusion.
They were days to cherish, pleasant
times. Song birds were still singing.
Everything about his world so special.
Sudden-shock! In truth, it was least
expected. As if a call came down, his
Father left the fold.
He cried, "What now?" Swiftly cried,
"Unknown!" Though ill winds shake
the trees, heart and mind still strong,
somehow, found the quiet, the calm.

He is older now, the winds are
silent. In truth, he knows what
dreams are made of. Moments,
he turns, gives thanks he found
happiness; his family, his family
of friends.
A wife, their bond still strong. Lo,
because of a Mother's wise words,
he grew the image of his Father's
ways. And what more can one say
about life? Oh, how fortunate, "The
Magic Of It All."

Why We Make The Tour

Walking my days, my nights, I wonder
on whose terms birds sing, rain pours,
thunder roars? How born a little child,
each new day a dream, each new day
a memory?
I see flowers, bees, how lonely winds
whisper the trees. And misty rain, the
green grass, white snow. Lo, think of
their purpose. Who can I call, who can
tell?
Aware, I am none of these, wonder who
am I? What of my purpose? So much
alive, yet, like all things, a body fading,
ends. I wonder, am I, all of us, slaves
to ignorance?
One day, like a box, hemmed in paper
brown, stored in the attic, lo, never to
be seen again. Was a little bird in song,
turn, listen, as life's precious moments
speak to me.
How our heart and mind play their part.
Oh, one precious thought: be aware we
all have a song to sing. Lo, somewhere
along the way, we are asked to sing our
song.
What gives us hope? One day, we stand,
silver trees among the hardwoods, little
old people. We ask, we leave this place.
Do we keep walking? What is truth?

It is of reason, I ask you to think.
What about the silence? Lo, we
live in light and darkness. And like
all things, we have learned to live
in thin air.
In truth, so much in life, feelings,
our thoughts and more, we can't
see or touch. Yet, we know when
they are there.
Why we must never forget life's
golden door of hope. "Why We
Make The Tour?" Oh people, tell
me, without hope, what have we?

Old Oak Farm

Perhaps, the lonely sound, bells drifting
across the green, takes away his years.
Memories rise, the house, Chapel, where
in every heart a sigh, in every heart there
is a song.
Little boy running free, little birds upon
a tree, brook close by. Lo, how splendor
falls, new greening of the wood. When
winds blow down, red leaves, the green,
the gold, their silhouettes, cover all the
ground.
Like lights go on, go off, foliage changes,
lo, white snow covers the ground. Snake
hill, little boy, his sleigh, twisting, turning,
sliding down. No doubts, no alarms, none
but laughter, laughter at "Old Oak Farm."
Softly, softly, now the winds, mirror on the
lake smiled at him.
His heart sings. "Can you see, this is your
world?" One precious moment captured
life's grace, the smile upon his face. So
happy the songs they sing and how they
all laugh. He sighed, "Oh, life, you are so
much more than a dream."
Sudden-like, he realized how time called
his name, he turned and bowed his head.
Suddenly speaks, "Oh, life, I shall never
forget, in your silence you spoke to me."

Happened, the afterglow, family,
friends, gathered all round, smiles.
Speaks, "Oh, people, one day time
will take away your years. Oh, one
wish, comes your time, you look
back upon your memories, those
of which you are so fond.
You will find your "Old Oak Farm."
The force, the stability, the power
that will continue to brighten and
give life to your world.

Keep On Dancing

Why does a little bird sing?
And the wind, rain, the sun, moon, the
stars? Oh, about life itself? Each step
we take, why bathed in silence? Oh,
what of our doubts, our fears? Are they
yours or mine? Or do they belong to
all of us?
We enter this world, passengers upon
streets of time, ask, "Who are we? Why
are we here?" And what shame, once
sadness calls, restricts our legacy, how
we cater to life's pleasures. Lo, life was
made to wander! Why not let it wander
as it will? "Keep On Dancing."
Our path, a pilgrimage through time, let
not your heart remain dormant. Oh, let
resolve confront the storms within us.
Smile at the rain, laugh with the snow
man, chuckle as you ride winds of time.
Ah yes, long as life's music plays, let
us "Keep On Dancing."
Once our emotions are positive, why
not catch a falling star, challenge your
name. And as Autumn leaves begin to
fall, scatter and hide, old man winter
coming soon. Aware our mind moves
our body parts. Why not "Keep On
Dancing?"

Oh, listen, listen, despite life's highs
and lows, we live free, as free can
be. Such, give credence to silvery
tones, a poet's voice. Oh, can you
see, our life was made for living.
And can you, me, anyone, see life's
future? Such, let us chase away our
fears, cry one wish, "I will live, I will
never give up! Ah yes, I will "Keep
On Dancing!"

Reflections In A Country Garden

Was a Sabbath morn, after reading
of the Psalms, Father and son were
enjoying their country garden. Lazy
winds whisper the trees, a little
bird sings. The young man asks
 an age old question, "Why do
little birds sing?"
His look, of deep concern, Father
speaks.
"Some say because they are happy.
Some because they are sad. And others,
because they have a song to sing.
My son, let us look at this world of ours."
The never ending sky, lo, unlimited
space and the multitude, the crowds
of people. We ask, where does our
path end? Here or in silent corridors
of time? And men, women, all ages,
how none look alike, Nor know, why
we are here or who we are?
My son, there is so much we want
to know. How winds blow down, our
days turn into nights. Why we love.
We laugh, we cry. Ah, yes, what of a
great mystery power? Why poets
continue to raise their pen, ask the
reason, the how and the why.

As if a call came down, Father
turns, tells life is like a book.
Once we turn the pages, find
life is a mystery, life is beauty.
Life is our greatest gift.
Thereto, life is fragile, life is of
happiness. Perhaps, how best
we define our success. Lo, until
we find the answers, let us open
our eyes to life's grace. The tie
that binds all of us; lo, our family,
our family of friends.

The Hill Birds Sing

First threads of morning light, life he
finds, where barley fields scatter the
edge of forest green. A morn, the hill
birds in song, vary beats of his heart.
How soon, a mind in tune, he lets his
heart wander as it will.
He remembers how fast our years
unwind. How as a boy, thought as a
boy; now a man, speaks like a man.
Lo, was birth of a moment! He turns
to the genesis of all things; nature,
creatures, large and small.
Oh, one thing seems certain, the
people were made for each other.
Strikes his mind, how we bring both
good and evil. In the sum of life, all
things, surely, there is something
real going on.
Though man is measured by time,
bodies rise, bodies fall. Seems only
man was given the power to think,
to reason. Our grace, how we can
see all things through our constant
mind.
Of the story told, what touched him
most? Oh, a thing of beauty! One day
we are called upon to see all things,
through the beauty of our soul.

How subtle this life of ours. It was
sudden-like, hill birds sing again.
He remembered the story told of
a Prophet,
How we all walk a magic circle
we call life. Lo, Faith must be our
guide. How all will know thee.
He tells, when they call our name,
by our leave, we will hear a quiet
voice, "Welcome, build your house
here, the other side, where winds
blow down and lake water rides."

PART FOUR

Sonnet IV

River Runs Deep

Never the day, the winds doth blow,
Walks with me, the lonely sea, the sky.
I fail to remember, footsteps in the snow.
We laughed, we cried, my question, Why?

Come the snowflakes through the night,
Lo, her hollow footsteps mark the snow.
Paints forest green, picture, pearly white,
A body in motion, river runs deep below.

I hear my heart in calling, to understand,
I am here, she is there, a heart in sorrow.
The ice, the snow, why His Silent Hand?
Now who can tell about our tomorrows?

The ice was smooth, the river runs deep.
Lo, as the river flows, I continue to weep.

Time Shadows

Restless, paying homage to night's
darkness, I was touched by sounds
we feed upon, time, life, and though
skeptical, by our faith. Time shadows
how they continue to appear and test
our minds each day.
How we walk our way, weeks, years,
may be but a day. What is truth? Lo,
who can tell? Is our life planned line
by line? What mystic means cause
time spans in this life of mine? And
the science of our body, the ease
we walk our way.
The sun, moon, so perfect in their
distance, yet, so far away. Older
now, yet, I still pursue faith in One
divine. Has been my destined way.
Lo, lest one doubts a mind's intent,
my parents planted seed. "My son,
have pride in your noble deeds."
Listen, once a little child is found
wanting, no answer to find. Indeed,
disturbs time shadows of my mind.
How difficult the masquerade, be
not the tactless clown, ignore truth.
Lo, no answers can be found. I tie
this story to our name.

By our leave this place, can it be,
time renews itself, we are called
to walk upon a higher plain? Lo,
perhaps, why we walk, talk, were
given reason to think how and
why?
Why I will be bold, place my faith
in the greatest story ever told. Lo,
one happy day, life's Grace will
call my name, provide answers
to "Time Shadows" of my mind.

How Do I Know Love?

Alone with my thoughts, soft call of
the dove; soft call in return, touch me
our numberless years. Our wealth is
so bound to our feelings; days to trust,
to cherish. I cry loud and clear, "Oh,
love, how do I know thee?"
Looking back, like two young birds upon
a tree, see two hearts singing one song.
We played games young birds play, yet
we captured passion's pulse. Unlike the
hunter, found the recipe for self-control,
no broken promises.
How soon, whisper the winds, words of
which, only words of truth in love, dare,
tell. We laugh, we sing, we dance. Life
turning, turning, as if a call came down,
bound our two hearts.
Our grace, church, crowds of people.
How we never forget our vows taken,
promises we made. I tell thee now and
then again, we are so aware our life is
a short journey.
Such, we must never forget how two
happy hearts found truth in love. One
precious wish, "No broken wings and
no broken promises. And never forget,
to think, to act, as of all the world were
young."

It was the distant cry of the loon,
bubbly sounds of chattering brook.
Our house, where grass all round
seems painted shiny green.
I reflect upon our time, our family,
our family of friends. A mind can
see all these things. And perhaps,
of life, that is all we should ask.

Looking Glass Lake

It was from a high road, tall pines
reaching for the sky, golden lights,
the sun, sparkle reflections upon
lake water far below. I spy the old
church, vistas, green trees, fond
memories turn my mind.
I remember hidden, the woodland
setting, playmates found a secret
place. Where youthful blood grows
warm, their innocence feeds naivete
of youth. The meeting of the minds,
of two happy hearts.
They laugh, sing, shout, suddenly,
tightness of water-logged clothes,
stimulate outlines of desire. When
eyes meet, breath quickens, they
slosh ashore. Share idle talk, smile,
life's fancies charm their day.
Still moves time, now all grown up,
if one asks about first plunge into
"Looking Glass Lake," was I there?
Oh, shall I harbor silence or speak,
perhaps, stoop to folly? I ask, can
one be both judge and jury?
The sky, the gray clouds, hides the
sun, begin my long walk home. As
I have often done before, I prepare
for life's table of new tomorrows.

I often wonder the answer to my
questions. Whom shall I ask? Or,
is there an answer? Why not be
bold? I will judge not but call upon
life's splendor, forgiveness.
I remember how beautiful the view,
the reflections on "Looking Glass
Lake." Happy, I walk on, smile and
hum an old time tune.

To A Young Bride

My dear, you are so young; I, so bold.
How natural we stand at heart's length.
As I stroke your face, your hair, find so
much tenderness there. Oh, fear not,
walks our way, hands of love.
Like two trees, we stand face to face,
two hearts glide a meandering stream.
From depth of a whisper, the high of a
scream, our promise. Commitment to
each new wish, each new dream.
As I stroke your face, your hair, we
share heart's sweet song. I speak the
knot we tied, grace notes. Oh, sleep,
sweet sleep, my dear, it was destiny
called our names. Such, we embrace
our communion, lo, our two hearts life
bound.
Why our passion will feed time and will
chase careless youth. And fate will be
kind, be dear, will plant life's heartfelt
offerings. Lo, seeds that will feed love
and will bloom our togetherness.
My dear, one wish, please hear my call.
Like wild flowers, once winds blow down,
dance the hills of green. As long as life's
music plays, we will sing one song. "You
will never walk alone."

My dear, as we sail the river swift,
our life. Our ports of call, first, the
last, happiness, let us remember,
like the tide changes, water begins
to fall. How our life will change. Lo,
one morn, our day of no dawning!
I am prone to believe, the Captain
of the ship of life will call our name.
"Oh, how fortunate I have found two
happy hearts. Please come sail with
me."

Sir Knight

He called it a promise land, place
music plays, star lights shine, one
wish, catch a falling star. And then
dance wild and wooly free. Once
the band plays down, hold hands,
keep on smiling. Then play life's
game, comic sleep.
Oh, a night, he would break with
the past. He failed to promptly cry
goodbye. As if fire burns, embers
low, love and happiness played a
part. In truth, was something new
happening that morn.
Aware the road he travels, a road
without end. Tired of walking life's
empty corridors, he pledged his
devotion to youthful dreams. They
embraced charms of bondage. Lo,
two hearts became one.
Grows a well worn path, older now,
stand two trees close by, two birds
in song. Their grace, life's music is
still playing. Their lifetime? Oh, how
they danced!
Lo, it was a moment, so often has
happened before. Sudden-like, the
old clock upon the wall tolls, their
bodies stir.

Awake, she smiles, turns, puffs
her pillow. He adjusts her blanket,
covers her shoulder. A virtue that
cannot be ignored. Spins his mind,
how they danced a lifetime to the
same music man.
It was their devotion to truth, their
prayers were answered. How they
walked a well-worn path. Lo, their
grace! The night they cried, "Never
goodbye." I speak of the love affair
of Sir Knight and his lady fair.

The Way It Was

Perhaps, the gray dawn, sounds of
distant thunder, I crossed the winds
of time. Remember, a far off place,
little town, sweeps the world, winds
of war. Moments, two hearts meet,
like others have before, clasp hands.
So much within themselves ignore
all things, the guns, the doubts, their
fears.
Happens, the drums, bugles call his
name, soldier boy. Shock! What do
we do, the many questions? Tell me,
where are the answers? One often
wonders, perhaps, a quiet voice, we
find our strength; the truth in love, lo,
marriage, the effect!
Like winds blow down, he was called,
perhaps, leave for the little town. And
of those left behind, what renders pain,
ugliness, sacrifice. The wall between
their separation. Lo, their days in the
wilderness!
Sudden-like, the good news, the guns
are silent now. The bands play down,
slowly, slowly, the ugliness fades away,
And though tattered and torn, their two
hearts cry, "We will live again, our life
reborn."

In reflection, the way it was.
Oh, what greater faith, their
desire, ignore the rage of fire.
War!
And as so many others have
done before, two hearts share
the willingness to define their
love. They challenge the pace
of life.
What follows, fond memories
become treasures of their time,
and grow love the rest of their
lives.

Building Of The Nest

Happened early morn, crossing the
green. Out of the silence, the two of
them. We stand motionless and still.
Appearing, out of the pond weeds,
majestic, in their finery, red top, gray,
all found their piercing eyes, Sand
Hill Cranes.
Flapping wings, on spindly legs, two
bodies dancing, prancing, a wedding
song in their hearts. What inspired
us most, their feelings high, the birth
of a moment, fluffs of brown. Speaks
to me, what follows, parent's solitary
eyes upon them.
It will be only time that will unlock their
door. Their grace, like many a human
child, not until after the grooming, will
they fly away, fly away. What touched
our heart, our view, beauty of nature's
call. The bond of which I speak, life's
greatest feelings.
And what more do we ask of life than
love and affection? And far beyond all
things, as if out of stones of care, build
a house, a family. Why many a lonely
heart has never cried. Lo, they found
life's greatest gift! They found the way
to mate for life.

Oh, can you see, no greater thrill,
two hearts meet, find love is true.
Once life's music plays, their life
all in tune, define happiness and
success, drink champagne.
Oh, there is one thing we all dare
not forget: the telling reason for
our happiness, our success, found
in the pond weeds. "Building Of The
Nest."

A Little Girl Once Walking

We meet, though confined to a chair
that rides, she still wears a smile. Oh,
little girls were made to play a place
apart, dance lively steps, share happy
sounds. Aware life's promises may be
forever hidden from her view, wonder,
from where, from whom, will she find
her strength.
Our life is of many silent things. And
in every heart there is music, waiting
for a song to sing. Oh, who can tell
what or who will touch her heart and
give life to her world? Unanswered, I
turn, cry my deep concern.
Oh, life, you who know when sugar
maples ripen, flower petals fall, rain
pours, signal a rainbow cometh, Oh
can you tell from whom, from where
her happiness? Or is her smile, result
of the pageantry of illusion?
Moments, I feel soft arms around my
neck, her warmth, her love. How she
lives her loneliness, yet, still smiles.
Oh, I never dreamed of such things.
It came from the steeple tower, sound
of bells. Tells of a spirit within us, how
it touches our lives.

Oh, how my heart sings, I call her
name. My fair maid, I speak of you.
Can you see what you have done
for me?
Like the Heaven-born child, your
willing smile, your love turned my
life around. Through your spirit I
found happiness. I found purpose.
I found love.

The Christmas Tree

A quiet night, firelight twists, turns.
His eyes upon the window, moon's
bright beams of light shine upon
the wood. Quiet place, where the
old tree once stood. Ah yes, was
a picture of silent grace.
His thoughts mingling the ashes,
a dreamer cries, "How much the
tree like me." How seeds planted,
two trees grow close by. Lo, like a
man, a woman, tangled branches,
tiny knots, commitments.
Was destiny called their names,
like little birds, suddenly find their
wings, life's magic moments begin.
Looking back, how beautiful songs
they sing. Yet, it happens to all of
us.
Like tree branches hang low, our
bodies soon stoop in sigh. And the
nights grow cold, a mighty tree no
longer refuge to little birds, those
who cannot fly alone. And though
our spirit still fierce, we too, must
yield to the wish of time.
It was music of a little child's laugh,
turned his life around. The song he
sings about, "The Christmas Tree."

Oh, listen, listen, all you people in
my life of this story told. I sing to
all the world.
"Oh, Christmas tree, you are there
tonight, your candles burning very
bright. Yet, one day, we will look at
you on the ebb. A mass of needles,
a tangled web.
Alas, one day, you will be cast upon
the heap. Yet, our secret, you are
but asleep. For like all of us, you will
rise again, be a member of a family,
and surely find another friend."

Whispers In The Night

Oh, Bonnie, lass of love and beauty,
round and round we danced, tweedle
of bagpipes high. How soon, fancies
rise within us, we dance our reckless
hearts. How natural, a boy, a girl, we
pursue whispers in the night.
I will never forget our adventure, once
our feelings high, softly, softly, sound
your sweet words, "My dear, in you, I
place my trust." Happened, promises
of nature, beyond our control. Oh, so
alive, your melancholy; still remember
your tears.
Yet, Bonnie was not born to walk in
shadows of her fears. It was your
smile, your maiden form so round, so
gently pressed, your cry, "Oh, what do
I see, was love too much for me? Yet,
I'm laughing, I'm singing, I'm dancing
on a cloud." One precious moment,
our two hearts all in tune.
Lo, unchained, our love could not be
denied! Dear Bonnie, lass of love and
beauty, I no longer see your roguish
eye; see only two of us. And how life's
music plays the tweedle of bagpipes
high, whispers in the night.

Oh, as if a call came down, truth
entered the garden gate. Our vows,
the Deacon's smile, soft, gentle his
words.
"Oh, Dear Bonnie, lass of love and
beauty, dance the tweedles, of the
bagpipes high. Live the life you were
born to live." We were wed, surely,
Heaven was on our side.

When Heaven Calls Our Name

What is a life without a dream?
And how beautiful when dreams
come true? I speak of a man and
a woman. How echoes roll from
soul to soul. Once their promises
made, they share life's prevailing
beat.
Sunrise, sunset, turn to love they
love best. Oh, so much more than
passion, they capture the spirit of
true love. One precious day, birth
of a moment, something they will
never forget.
From a far off place, drifting winds,
sounds of life's music, little birds
sing. Flowers bob and weave, the
wind in their hair, trees kneel as if
in prayer. And little elves and fairies,
happily dance till dawn of the new
day.
Out of a beautiful rainbow, angels
sally forth and capture a shining star,
shower it with the sweetest things in
Heaven. Once wrapped in a blanket
of beautiful dreams. Upon receiving
God's blessing, silky clouds come
down, opens wide a path, a carpet
so fair, none can compare.

Softly, softly, life all quiet and still,
from a distance, humming sound;
bearers of glad tidings. Appearing,
chariot, pure gold, a host of angels
lead the way. In the spirit of desire,
they sing songs of praise and glory.
Oh, one precious moment, "When
Heaven Calls Our Name." On the
wings of angels, our little child was
born.

Harmony Of The Bells

They met, they danced, how soon
they captured fruits of life, church,
Deacon's words, rice spread forth
upon the ground. Like little birds in
song, their life was all in tune.
So much more than passion, truth
filled the air, grows a circle of love.
A family, confluence of friends, the
things that counted. Lo, it was least
expected! Called to leave, all cried,
"Too soon, too soon."
Now every Sunday, she stands by
his mourning stone. Once, sun high,
plays host to her heart, she speaks
to him, "My dear, I bless quiet lights
break of day. They unveil footsteps
upon dewy ground. My grace, I feel
your presence."
I will never forget the day she called
time. Perhaps, her fear, she asked
life's magic question, "Why does our
journey end? It breeds sadness and
deep discontent. Who can tell why
and who called his name?"
It happened, the steeple tower, as if
in answer, sound the bells and she
cried loud and clear, "One precious
wish."

"Oh, time, Once you ring my
bell, open my door, I leave for
the other time, the other place.
He and I will meet again."
She turns and neatly places
flowers into the ground; close
by, tiny flag flutters. She takes
my hand, waves her goodbye.
And o'er life's hallowed ground,
sound the bells, the harmony
of the bells.

Footsteps

A quiet night, restless night, comes
early morn, awake, mirror on the wall
speaks to me, "You have lived better
part of knowing time." Though I did
not breathe despair, I show my deep
concern, cry, "Who can tell where we
go from here?"
There have been stories told, some
call them fancies and some call them
make believe. Yet, how subtle silence
of the morn, unlocked images; beauty
of a dream. And I found the roots of
confidence. My thrill chased away all
my doubts, my fears.
From a distance hangs cloud of dust,
crowds of people following footsteps
of a Rabbi. His words soft, His motions
delicate, tells the earth, the sea have
boundary lines. How the ocean waves
rise, roll upon the sand, silently, return
to the sea.
Such, the people rise and fall, return
to a place of which our legends speak;
a quiet place where happiness dwells,
love is the first, is the last. Lo, our most
vital feeling. One precious moment, the
voice in the mirror whispers my name.

"Oh, can you see the miracle of our
world about; our time, space, and
motion? You would be a fool in your
heart if you ignored the truth.
What would our life be without His
promise?" Suddenly, my heart sings,
I smile again, turn to my constant
mind. Oh, so little He has asked of
me, no twists, no turns, the path He
walks. I will follow the footsteps of
the Rabbi.

Heaven's Watchful Eye

It was long ago, something she would
never forget. What touched her heart,
his warm feelings and his tenderness.
Oh, what could have been? And now,
the crown he wears, in her very own
church.
Little children, they played round the
willow tree. He smiled at her and she
smiled at him. He dared all to climb
the tree. Only he, only she climbed
the tree; so high, close by, Heaven's
Watchful Eye.
And they laugh together, they cried
together, their time together, none
but joy and happiness. Ah yes, they
were close, yet, somehow found the
way to stand apart. Sudden-like, his
lips unsealed, his destiny; his desire
to walk alone.
Oh, doubtful shadows touched her
wounded heart. The first time she
truly cried. They kept in touch, yet,
she often wondered, what causes
one to embrace hope, accept the
confessions of the heart, beauty of
the dream. Softly, the organ played,
people were stirring, were leaving
now.

In her goodbye, how he pressed
her hand, she knew the bridge
was still there. Oh, one precious
moment, their time came back to
her.
No longer a doubtful heart but a
new understanding of her treetop
partner, man of the cloth. Lo, the
spirit within him, a heart that cares!
Though he may walk alone, now a
partner to "Heaven's Watchful Eye,"
he will never be lonely.

Welcome To The Dance

Her dress, her casual walk, confident
glance, whatever desire he ever had,
had come to the dance. He was from
Swagger town, pompous air, spirit of
youth, his body swings and sways as
the music plays.
While sounds of thunder howl distant
shores, ever louder than before. The
fates were stirring there, were coming
to the dance. The band played, they
dance with carefree hearts, immune
to thunder, guns, the cries, and all the
body parts.
Music soft and low, bodies swing and
sway, emotions flow. Yet, the fates had
come to the dance that day. And they
marched, the planes, the ships, upon
distant shores; would have their way.
And ever louder than before, distant
thunder roars.
Aware destiny will call their names,
yet, two hearts clasp hands. And their
trial begins; he leaves for the distant
lands. Oh, it was not in her mind to
hide from fears of yesterday; tomorrow
was her concern. The letter came, the
greatness, sacrifice the Swagger town
guy. Yet, the flag still flies, half-mast
high.

Oh, let us shout courage to them
all. Yet, let us all look behind the
memories that hang upon life's
door. Who can tell, what means
it all?
They cry, "War, never again!" Oh,
did they lie? For in circle round,
bands play, tunes we have heard
before; and they march, the ships,
planes, near or distant shores. Lo,
why I ask again and again! "After
they fall, who can tell, what means
it all?"

Saturday Night Tears

Gray dawn, a wind that chills a last
goodbye, she stood as if in a waste
land. Oh, it was so hard to believe
he was silenced forevermore. Time
turned, her lonely nights were hard
to bear. Mother, now cleaning lady,
the house we share.
Looking back, seems a thousand
times, bagging, dragging, carry our
clothes down. We move to another
new place, to another new town.
I speak of a Mother's cry, "My son,
I so often feel like a fool, our move
another new place, And you, off to
another new school."
Ugly, the city, no car, no bus or no
train; long walk to school, cries the
rain. A little boy no one knows, sits
in his water-logged clothes. And I,
remember meeting, passing, each
new day, the same, how time called
our name. Oh, be bold, love to have
and to hold.
How two hearts learned, hold back
your tears and laugh off your fears.
I remember life's music played, my
new surprise, her smile, happiness,
the smile in her eyes.

He was charming, his grace,
sadness leaves her face. And
I pack my clothes and move
to another new place. Listen,
the end of this story told.
I remember the softness and
the gleam in her eye, explains
our move and the reason why.
Ah yes, I remember the tears,
"Saturday Night Tears," a night
Mother no longer cried.

Shadows Of Darkness

His eyes wide open, yet, he cannot
see. Young man, not fragile, energy
still there. Yet, tied down, destined to
walk shadows of darkness, His plight,
roots of uncertainty.
If one cared, could hear his cry, deep
distress. His grace, comfort, Mother's
words, "Oh, can you see how much
he trembles?" Strong, stern, speaks
of the art of living.
How a shepherd boy became a King.
How people will amaze once they
hear your cry, "A useless soul am I,
if I do not try." Surely then, they will
rise, find a way to share their labor
and their trust.
He listened, he learned, time turned
the hour glass. It was from wisdom
of a Mother's words, found a willing
heart, willing mind. He challenged
paths he walked.
Slowly, silently, rides the waves like
a sailing ship. Sailing, sailing, dark
clouds rising, blanket the night. Lo,
he found how life has its own way
of speaking.

He is older now and though he
walks in darkness, he walks a
winding path. His white tip cane,
will take him far as he can go.
Oh, something we should never
forget, the wisdom of a Mother's
words.
"Son, reflect upon your dreams,
let your attitude be your guiding
light, and let your visions be your
sight." Listen, all you people in my
life: can you see how a Mother's
words set him free?

Our Country Place

Once reduced to walking calming
hours of the morn, something all
of us must remember. Time has
its own way of speaking. Let me
tell my story.
Awake, I walk backyard country,
my time clock, Old Red, barnyard
King. Though tired, weary, once
he calls, my morning chore, egg
gathering.
I cross the green, moments, early
morn becomes a scandal, stealing
of eggs. Lo, how soon the cackling
disturbs the hen house! I move fast,
the basket, the back door.
Swiftly, enter the family room, await
morning ritual, aroma of the coffee
bean. She enters, two cups, pours
the coffee. We are prone to speak
of the good old days; even hum old
time tunes.
Stories we tell, we tell again, seldom
will our mood change. Happy in our
state of mind, songs we sing, vows
we made. How we danced our life
through. Oh, we will never forget
where life's happiness dwells. Two
of us, living our life in togetherness.

Aware, we walk the edge of time,
when sadness touches us. Lo, we
remember all the good things: the
grace of life, love we receive from
our family, a call, a visit, perhaps
a letter from a friend.
We remember the places we lived,
songs we sang. Lo, how we danced!
Once awake, the morning sun, the
eggs, the coffee. Oh, how fortunate
we have been, our two hearts still
in love, here in "Our Country Place."

Miss Bess

Happened, where the beat goes on.
Clad in beauty of the night, her swish,
her sway, like a flower dancing in the
wind. Though her fragrance false,
we find coy excuse, we sin and then
we laugh.
Oh, Miss Bess, as if music fills the air,
your sweet strains bring sunshine to
a lonely heart. Yet, your wild cadence,
your thrill, brings inevitable sadness.
Once, the beat is over, you smile and
silently steal away.
Lo, so my need, melancholy lingers,
fond memories are too delicious to
be absent from my heart. Why each
eye cries a tear, why I call your name.
"Miss Bess, please hear me, aware
it's not true love we share, yet, of you,
I will never forget."
Though walls of separation between
us, I still see thee as a flower. In truth,
not a blushing flower. Your glitter is in
gold. Yet, your devotion to this lonely
heart, I ask, "Oh, who are we? Who am
I, anyone to judge?"
And though many may never accept
your way, my sense, power of reason.
My dear, what slight need I forgive?

Our steps crimson, yet, we are so
close, one step away; two hearts
lonely. Like the muffled sounds of
earth, let the past be the past. Let
us join hands, marriage the effect.
One precious wish, His judgment
be kind.
Oh, hard to believe it happened, we
found the way, crossed the bridge; we
found something greater than most.
No cries, no sighs, we live our life
the way life intended it to be lived.

Love Grows A Beautiful Evening

Dear Children, our new day dawns,
we still choose the games we play.
Seldom, speak of idle hours, yet not
too far away. Oh, this feeling, we cry
one wish, "How best to catch time, a
thief."
Lo, we are thinking of you, your day.
Aware life's grace, where the heart
is, spins our mind, the sound of your
voice. Rise feelings, ne'er had before.
Our wish, your steps close by. Listen,
hear our call.
As if new buds in our garden grow,
our happiness, we will be with you.
How beautiful, when present and
past meet. Lo, our thrill, memories,
how tender the night. Heaven calls
your name. Oh, how nothing else
matters.
Our world comes alive again, paints
a picture. Our life, our time, how soft
the night, our two hearts found truth
in love. You were born. Time turns,
now all grown up, church, steeple,
the crowds of people.
Though you too found truth in love,
we found life's grace. You never
forget us once you call our name.
Lo, love grows, a beautiful evening.

Oh, listen, our days may turn ashen
gray, rain may bar our way. I speak
of life's grace, why we remember
youth, your vows.
A Mother's approving eyes, Father's
warm heart. How it was, how it still
is. Our decades, decades, time, our
wandering days.
We look out the windows of time.
One precious wish: Our eyes upon
you and your little ones, our family.
Your call, a note, a visit. Lo, when
"Love Grows A Beautiful Evening."

Mourning Rose

A thing of beauty, the story he told
how they found their happiness in
a country garden. Where bees wear
a crown, one touch, lo, opens wide
flowers of summertime. How did it
happen? No warning sign, suddenly,
a loving heart, quiet and still.
Now, she rests a place apart, in our
garden near. Stands a mighty tree,
as if a sentinel to guard her. Oh, the
futility he bares, so near, yet, so far,
he knows not where. A morn, the
song birds sing.
Loud and clear, here is what heard:
"Please, do not flow your precious
tears. A rose is a rose. It will bloom
again a flower in summertime." Lo,
his fear of losing her, turns suddenly,
realizes how a body clings to earth.
How our soul stands alone, follows
its own identity.
How sweet the dream, he can see the
beauty of it all, measures the moment.
How like silence of the night, how close
we are to peace. How we rest in quiet
sleep. Happened, summer sun, in our
garden near.

Sun's ribbons of light shine upon
her leafy nest. He remembers the
story told, how we will meet again.
He kneels, bows, faith kneels by
his side.
Oh, can you see, softly, silently,
how love dwells in our garden?
Her color, burning bright, velvet
soft, her touch. Lo, let us bless
flowers of summertime. My rose
in bloom still grows.

Grace Notes

Time is a subtle thing, a silent thing,
slowly, slowly, turns days, our nights.
One day, mirror on the wall tells, "You
are older now." What else but appeal
to time as King. "Oh, time, where do
you lead me?"
We live near the water marsh, where
icons of old age gather together, track
memory patterns; their victories, their
unplanned defeats, once a Prince of
song, Queen of the dance. Yet, still
proud, the currents of their time.
And though they left their temptations
behind, form a magic circle, find ways
that lead to happiness. One will cry a
little, one will laugh a little, and some
will sing old time tunes. Togetherness,
calls their name.
Lo, like birds step lightly on the grass,
they walk. Never forget to stop, tell bits
and pieces of their life's story. If nothing
else, continue to dream. Ah yes, let it be
known, they built their house, their lives
with stones of care.
Though time has turned desires, their
visions waiver in the shade. Lo, time's
gift to all of us, a blessing made. How
beautiful the life we live.

I speak, how life continues, we walk
together, we talk together. Oh, voice
to voice, chatter, chatter, what keeps
our world alive.
Oh, people, what more dare we ask
of life? No longer the loneliness, the
watchful waiting. How beautiful, once
the heart sings, "Grace Notes." The
place I live, I am no longer alone. Lo,
a place I can call my home..

Milestones

My comfort chair, listening to the song
she sings, I realize, how I never tire of
my playmate's voice. Opens my mind
memories, how we met, capture life's
most precious moments.
How we walked the aisle, two happy
hearts. How we followed the sun, walk
life's roadside trails, sing, dance, time's
elegance. Our grace, we sing one song,
togetherness.
One precious morn, born a little child,
tiny fingers, smiling eyes. Like coo of
a dove, born family sounds. Lo, our life
in change. We build a house, a family,
new friends, "Milestones."
We give thanks to Heaven's Watchful
Eye. How He marked our path with His
applause. "Though our path is well
traveled, you have kept promises you
were asked to keep."
Oh, how we smiled, sing heart's sweet
song. How this life, all things became
companion to our time, all because of
life's most precious words, "I—Love—You."
We often wonder from where the voice
we heard, "What gives you your strength
to reach end of the road? "Milestones."

Listen, seldom can life's fields of
happiness be sustained, once we
fail to bring happiness into our lives.
How do we do this?
Building, what gives all of us reason
to share our victories and unplanned
defeats. Building with stones of care,
"Milestones." And the greatest of all
is love.

The Invitation

Happens to all of us, yet, so difficult to
accept and some prefer to ignore reality.
Yet, time has a dialogue all its own. Her
eyes bright, how she stared at pictures
on the wall, tell her story.
Still feisty, it was not in her to accept
change. Lo, I ask, how can life be so
dear, yet, be so unkind? How one day,
we call, ask one to leave their home
for another place to stay.
We walk room to room, found chairs
were old, rugs were frayed, the plants
were dying. And her pet canine, in a
steady limp around the room. Yes, it
was her time; it had to be done.
By our leave, hugs, the kisses, oh, so
anxious, we did everything we could.
Oh, one precious wish, time becomes
her friend. Yes, there was something
more.
Aware, one day soon, not too far away,
a call will come down, her journey will be
ending. Oh, each new day, our promise,
keep in touch. And so, as we stand apart,
like a lonely sea, 'neath a lonely sky; one
day, it happened. I heard a voice I heard
before calling me. I remember the laughs,
the tears.

"Thank you, I am happy here.
One more thing, remember the
house by the shore? How silent
the sun, the stars? How soft, the
waves roll upon the sand?"
Oh, listen, I have found there
is beauty in silence. And I have
been told, one day, I will depart
for a more beautiful place. Lo,
a silent place! I will let you know.
"Oh, one day, why not you? Yes,
one day, you come too."

Dear Children

Hour upon hour, sit my comfort chair,
measure our days, our nights. Eyes
upon our magic circle, see none but
silver gray heads. I almost cry, mirror
on the wall, the face I see no longer
belongs to me.
It was morning sun, how high ribbons
of light sparkle. I realized, something
new here this day. Morning shadows
come alive and random thoughts play
host to my mind. I realize time is my
prize.
Lo, I remember the day faith became
truth; the tie that binds happiness to
every day of our lives. The church, we
agree to walk together, heart to heart.
We found life's greatest gift, love and
affection.
Dear children, we all live our lives in a
frame of time. And time nourishes our
soul. Once faith is no longer a debate,
we find life's treasure—commitment. Oh,
how fortunate can we be!
As we walk life's roadside trails, often
the least expected happens. No warning
signs, lights upon our path may go dim.
Our dreams shattered, softly, softly, our
midnight hours call, "Come walk with me."

What speaks to me, once found
love and affection. What stronger
faith need we embrace than rage
of desire, our hearts on fire.
Then, two willing hearts, find ways
to challenge the pace of time. Oh,
never weaken, play games behind
life's curtain.
Build your house of stones of care;
Ever aware, happiness will follow,
long as your house stands on solid
ground, truth in love.

Like Leaves That Fall

As sun's ribbons of light play upon the
church window, the organ's soft chords
bleed. I retreat to a memory I will never
forget. The day we met, my knuckles
bare from the pleadings.
A moment's breath, life's music plays,
two hearts share a thousand blended
notes, love's delights. As if a call from
afar, love grows and grows. Lo, never
a bond more true. Love marks our path,
"You are the only one for me."
We cry one wish, our feelings continue
to grow. Like beauty of a rose, poetry
the prose, we travel life's highways full
circle. Our grace, how time honors our
days, our nights. Oh, how did we sing
our praises best?
Our feelings, how they moved our lives
each day. As if theater on the round, as
if lights go on, lights go off. Speaks to us,
the glamour, the beauty of the show. Ah
yes, how important the play, the strength
of the cast.
Why I show concern, the silence, end of
the play. We stand alone, none but fond
memories. Ask life's magic question, "Oh
where do we go from here?"

A modern man, a pragmatic man,
what lingers my mind, the beauty
of it all. Yet, the mystery of it all.
Oh, can it be, we live this life all in
vain?
Oh, can it be, we will meet again?
Like "Leaves That Fall," we leave
this place. Takes my hand, a very
Holy Face, leads me to a comfort
chair where all my riches lie, my
poet's pen.
Found the greatest secret of them
all: our life, there is no ending call!

In Call To Close

A few moments each day, take
heed, our cities, towns, country
places, voice of a little child. How
beautiful, sounds of innocence.
And how to each, with our hands
we give. And giving is where our
riches are.
A few moments each day, think of
family, friends, relationships. How
our feelings rise and fall. And how
they crown our hearts and minds,
move our lives each day.
A few moments each day, why not
give praise to all things that mark
our path, "I—love—you." For love is
our most vital feeling. And misty
rain, golden sun, what makes our
flowers grow. Snow, how it paints
forest green, pearly white.
And life's grace, ways and means,
many choices life offers. Oh, let us
think of life, our world about, take a
moment, the story told. The birth of
a beautiful garden and placed in the
center, presence of man.
A few moments each day, let us all
pray, we live a garden of hope. Yet,
whatever life's answer may be, let
us give thanks for our few moments
each day.

Charles P. Russ, Jr.

IN APPRECIATION

As we walk life's paths, how
soon we realize our happiness
comes through the "You Attitude."
Life is about others, not all about
me. Thus, my appreciation to Dr.
Charles E. Cravey—poet, author,
publisher, minister. His ear, his
interest, his dedication.
And to all those who review, read,
judge and comment on my books.
It is through their interest and
dedication that makes this book
possible.
Thanks.

Previous Books by the Author:

To Be Remembered

Love Has An Affair With Life

Life Notes

Songs of An Old Man